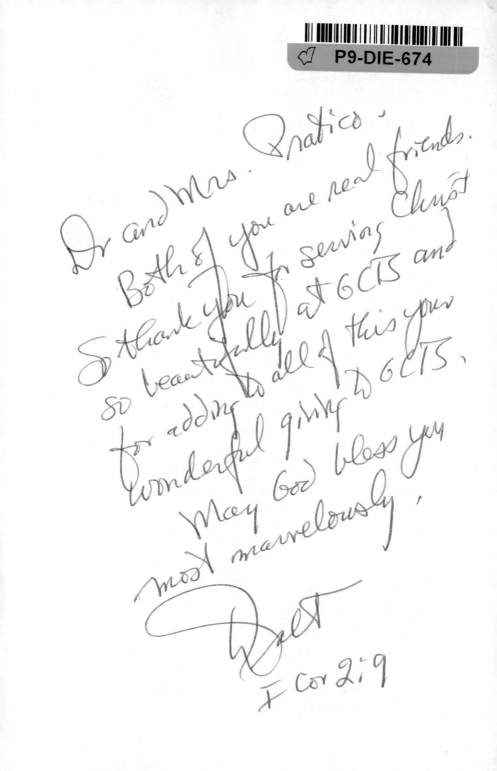

Dr. and Mrs. Pratico,
Both of you are real friends.
So thank you for serving Christ
so beautifully at GCTS and
for adding to all of this your
wonderful giving to GCTS.
May God bless you
most marvelously.

Walt

I Cor 2:9

Other books by Walter C. Kaiser, Jr.

MORE

HARD SAY- INGS

OF THE

OLD TESTAMENT

Walter C. Kaiser, Jr.

INTERVARSITY PRESS
DOWNERS GROVE, ILLINOIS 60515

InterVarsity Press is the book-publishing division of InterVarsity Christian Fellowship, a student movement active on campus at hundreds of universities, colleges and schools of nursing in the United States of America, and a member movement of the International Fellowship of Evangelical Students. For information about local and regional activities, write Public Relations Dept., InterVarsity Christian Fellowship, 6400 Schroeder Rd., P.O. Box 7895, Madison, WI 53707-7895.

Cover illustration: Dian Ameen-Newbern

ISBN 0-8308-1748-4

Printed in the United States of America ∞

Library of Congress Cataloging-in-Publication Data

Kaiser, Walter C.
   More hard sayings of the Old Testament/by Walter C. Kaiser, Jr.
     p.   cm.
    Includes index.
    ISBN 0-8308-1748-4
    1. Bible. O.T.—Criticism, interpretation, etc. I. Title.
   BS1171.2.K263 1992
   221.6—dc20   91-32389
                                               CIP

17	16	15	14	13	12	11	10	9	8	7	6	5	4	3	2
06	05	04	03	02	01	00	99	98	97	96	95	94	93		

Dedicated to
Mrs. Sophie Fletcher
and
Mrs. Marie Cosgrove
—two wonderful aunts
who have prayed, helped and given
generously
over the years
Psalm 125:4

Introduction: Recent Works on Bible Difficulties

More Hard Sayings of the Old Testament is intended to be a companion volume to *Hard Sayings of the Old Testament*. There was such an overwhelmingly positive response to that first book, both in sales and in requests for solutions to hard sayings not treated there, that the publisher and I have decided to offer a second contribution to the growing library of books now known as the Hard Sayings series.

In my first volume, I said that I would enjoy hearing from readers if there were additional sayings they wished had been addressed. Many of you did write, and I have tried to respond to all those requests in this companion volume. I want to express my appreciation to all who took the time to write and to express comments and questions.

Before we launch into this second set of sixty-eight hard sayings, perhaps it would be helpful if we reviewed some of the background studies on the nature, origin and reasons for biblical discrepancies.

Any observant Bible reader who compares statements of the Old Testament with those of the New Testament, statements of different writers within either testament, or even at times different passages within the same book will notice that there are apparent discrepancies. These statements, taken at face value, seem to contradict one another.

The Christian church has held over the centuries that there is an essential unity of the Holy Scriptures, that they form a divine library that is consistent and unified in its approach and teaching. Alas, however, as the scope of lay readership and the depth of scholarship have increased, an ever-increasing supply of alleged discrepancies and hard sayings has demanded attention.

Why are there so many discrepancies and difficulties? There are a great number of sources to which we can trace them: errors of copyists in the manuscripts that have been handed down to us; the practice of using multiple names for the same person or place; the practice of using different methods for calculating official years, lengths of regencies and events; the special scope and purpose of individual authors, which sometimes led them to arrange their material topically rather than chronologically; and differences in the position from which an event or object was described and employed by the various writers. All of these factors, and more, have had a profound influence on the material. Of course, to those who participated in the events and times these factors were less of a barrier than they are to us. Our distance from the times and culture exacerbates the difficulty. Specific issues might be mentioned here as illustrations of the wider field of difficulties. For example, the present Hebrew text of 1 Samuel 13:1 is a classic illustration of an early copyist's error that has continued to be unsolved to the present day. Literally, the Hebrew text reads: "Saul was a year old ['son of a year' in Hebrew] when he began to reign and two years he reigned over Israel." It is clear that the writer is following the custom of recording the monarch's age when he took office, along with the total number of years that he reigned. But it is also clear that the numbers have been lost and that this omission is older than the Greek Septuagint translation, made in the third century B.C. So far the Dead Sea Scrolls and all other ancient manuscripts have left us without a clue as to what the text should read.

The selectivity of the writers, in accord with their purposes in writing, can be illustrated from the genealogy that appears in Exodus 6:13-27. Instead of listing all twelve sons of Jacob, the writer is content to treat Reuben (v. 14), Simeon (v. 15) and Levi (vv. 16-25). Here he stops, even though he has listed only the first three sons of Jacob, because the sons of Levi, and particularly his descendants Moses and Aaron, are his special interest. So he does not proceed further.[1]

In treating some of these issues, I have chosen not to focus on points of tension that arise from such factual elements as time, history, culture and science. Instead, I have listened for points of tension in doctrine and ethics within the books or between authors of the Bible. I have included a few illustrations of difficulties having to do with facts, but my main emphasis is on theological and ethical questions.

In the previous volume I gave a brief history of works on biblical discrepancies up to the modern era. The subject has had an honored place throughout the history of the church, beginning with the church fathers, and in more recent days there has been a steady flow of contributions to this time-honored topic. Perhaps a listing of a few of them will aid the reader who wishes to continue studying these issues, or who desires to compare my solutions with those of others in the body of Christ.

In the last forty years, the most notable contributions to this subject have been the following. In 1950, George W. DeHoff wrote *Alleged Bible Contradictions* (Grand Rapids: Baker). He dealt with the subject by taking pairs of apparently opposing texts, which he grouped under the topics of systematic theology, ethics and historical facts. This work was followed in 1951 by the reissue of John W. Haley's 1874 text *An Examination of the Alleged Discrepancies of the Bible* (Nashville: B. C. Goodpasture). This was perhaps the most complete array of brief explanations of discrepancies; they were arranged under the divisions of doctrinal, ethical and historical discrepancies. A detailed first section treated the origin, design and results of the difficulties alleged to be found in the Bible.

In 1952 Martin Ralph De Haan published his *508 Answers to Bible Questions* (Grand Rapids: Zondervan). It included a mixture of doctrinal, factual and interpretive questions.

J. Carter Swaim contributed *Answers to Your Questions about the Bible* in 1965 (New York: Vanguard). Most of his text dealt with questions of fact rather than interpretation. Later, in 1972, F. F. Bruce published a volume entitled *Answers to Questions* (Grand Rapids: Zondervan). With only thirty-eight pages dealing with questions from the Old Testament, this work was divided into questions about Scripture passages and other matters related to the faith. In 1979, Robert H. Mounce contributed a book with a similar title, *Answers to Questions about the Bible* (Grand Rapids: Baker). His book had an unusually complete table of contents and dealt with a rather large number of difficulties for such a fairly brief work.

Paul R. Van Gorder added a text in 1980 called *Since You Asked* (Grand Rapids: Radio Bible Class). He organized his book alphabetically by topic and included a scriptural and topical index that gave a quick overview of the areas covered.

My colleague Gleason L. Archer produced a large tome in 1982 entitled *Encyclopedia of Bible Difficulties* (Grand Rapids: Zondervan). His arrangement followed the order of the biblical books as they appear in the canon. It included a mixture of issues such as authorship of the biblical books, critical objections to some of the books and alleged contradictions and problematical interpretations.

The first in the Hard Sayings series appeared in 1983. F. F. Bruce wrote *The Hard Sayings of Jesus* (Downers Grove, Ill.: InterVarsity Press). He took up seventy sayings of Jesus that were considered "hard" either because we cannot handily interpret them or because they seem so easy to interpret that their application is puzzling.

In 1987 David C. Downing published *What You Know Might Not Be So: 220 Misinterpretations of Bible Texts Explained* (Grand Rapids: Baker). Downing concentrated mainly on the confusion that exists between biblical passages and extrabiblical literature, myths and popular religions.

The second in the Hard Sayings series appeared in 1988—the companion to this present book, *Hard Sayings of the Old Testament* (Downers Grove, Ill.: InterVarsity Press). It addressed seventy-three difficult interpretation problems in the Old Testament. This work was quickly followed by Manfred T. Brauch's *Hard Sayings of Paul* (Downers Grove, Ill.: InterVarsity Press) in 1989; he took up four dozen texts from the Pauline corpus and sought to give a solution to the issues they raise. Shortly before Brauch's work appeared, Robert H. Stein produced a text entitled *Difficult Passages in the Epistles* (Grand Rapids: Baker, 1988). His arrangement was fivefold: understanding words, understanding grammar, understanding context, understanding content and understanding a pair of difficult passages using the comparative method. In 1991 Peter H. Davids explained seventy-two *More Hard Sayings of the New Testament* (Downers Grove, Ill.: InterVarsity Press).

Certainly, this is not a comprehensive list by any means, but it does demonstrate that the subject has continued to arouse keen interest over the years. My own contribution has focused particularly on interpretive issues of exegesis, hermeneutics, morality and theology. It is hoped that this book will prove as helpful to as many as the previous one evidently was.

I pray that this volume may encourage renewed enthusiasm for reading and studying the rich resources of the Old Testament. If only a few impediments to appreciating and utilizing the Old Testament are removed through this book, it will have been more than worth all the effort that has gone into it.

A special note of appreciation must go to my wife Marge for her help at various stages in the writing of this volume and for being a wonderful companion and friend in our joint calling to ministry. Likewise, I am deeply grateful for the way my administrative assistant, Mrs. Lois Armstrong, has continued to serve with me. She shouldered heavy administrative tasks in such an efficient way that I was able to squirrel away the hours required for writing this volume. It is also a pleasure to acknowledge the assistance and able editorial direction of James Hoover, managing editor at InterVarsity Press, and Ruth Goring Stewart, the copy editor. Their encouragement and sense of demanding excellence have added to whatever strengths this book possesses.

Note

[1]For a fuller treatment, see my commentary "Exodus," in *Expositor's Bible Commentary* (Grand Rapids: Zondervan, 1990), 2:344-45.

• C H A P T E R 1 •

The Lord Looked with Favor on Abel and His Offering

In the course of time Cain brought
some of the fruits of the soil as an offering
to the LORD. But Abel brought fat portions
from some of the firstborn of his flock.
The LORD looked with favor on Abel and his offering.
GENESIS 4:3-4

Does God have favorites? Does he show partiality for one over another—in this case, Abel over Cain? And does God prefer shepherds to farmers? If not, what was the essential difference between these first two sacrifices in the Bible?

Is the traditional interpretation correct in saying that the difference between Cain and Abel is only that one offered a bloody sacrifice and the other did not? If this understanding is correct, why are neither we nor they given any specific instructions to that effect? Up to this point, that distinction had not been made. And even if a distinction between the use and absence of blood was in vogue at this early date, why are both sacrifices referred to throughout this whole narrative with the Hebrew term *min-hah*, a "gift" or "meal offering"?

The answers to these questions are not as difficult as they may appear at first blush. There is only one overriding point on which there can be legitimate puzzlement: nothing in this episode indicates that this is the inauguration of the sacrificial system. While it does appear that this is the first time anyone ever sacrificed anything, the text does not specifically say so. That will remain, at best, only an inference.

Actually, the supposition that Cain and Abel's father, Adam, originated sacrifices may be closer to the truth, since no command authorizing or requesting sacrifices appears in these first chapters of Genesis. The whole subject of the origins of sacrifice is one that scholars have debated long and hard. Yet for all our work, the subject remains a mystery.

Even with this much caution, we must be careful about importing back into the times of Adam and Eve the instructions that Moses was later given on sacrifices. The word used to describe "sacrifice" throughout this episode of Cain and Abel is the word used in the broadest sense, *minhah*. It covers any type of gift that any person might bring. Consequently, the merit one gift might have over another does not lie in the content or type of gift—including the presence or absence of blood.

Of course, there was a problem with Cain's "gift"; but *he* was the problem. Genesis 4:3 describes how Cain merely brought "some" of the fruits of the field. Nothing can be said about the fact that he, as an agriculturalist, naturally brought what farmers have to give. But when his offering is contrasted with Abel's, a flaw immediately shows up.

Abel gave what cost him dearly, the "fat pieces"—in that culture considered the choicest parts—of "the firstborn" of his flock. Abel could very well have rationalized, as we might have done, that he would wait until some of those firstborn animals had matured and had one, two or three lambs of their own. Certainly at that point it would have been possible to give an even larger gift to God, and Abel would have been further ahead as well. Nevertheless, he gave instead what cost him most: he gave the "firstborn."

The telltale signs that we are dealing here with a contrast between formalistic worship and true worship of God are the emphasis that the text gives to the men and the verb it uses with both of them. In Genesis 4:4-5, there are four emphatic marks used with reference to the two brothers.

Literally, the Hebrew of verses 4 and 5 say: "And Abel, he brought, indeed, even he, some of the firstlings of his flock and some of the fat portions belonging to him. And the Lord regarded with favor Abel and [then] his offering. But unto Cain and [then] unto his offering, he did not have regard."

Clearly the focus of this passage is on the men. There are four emphatic elements in the text that mark this emphasis: first, the man's name, then the verb for "bringing" with the pronominal suffix, then the emphasizing particle *gam*, and finally the personal independent pronoun. It is difficult to see how the writer could have made it any more pointed that it was the men, and their heart's condition, that was the determinative factor in God's deciding whose sacrifice was to be accepted. The text almost stutters: "And Abel, he, he also, he brought."

The verb *sha'ah* means "to gaze," but when it is used with the preposition *'el* ("unto" or "toward"), as it is here, it means "to regard with favor." Ever since Luther, commentators have noticed that God's favor was pointedly directed toward the person first and then, and only then, toward the offering that person brought. Accordingly, this became the determinative factor in all worship: the heart attitude of the individual. If the heart was not found acceptable, the gift was likewise unacceptable.

It is true that an old Greek translation of this text rendered *sha'ah* in Greek as *enepyrisen*, "he kindled." Apparently the translator wanted to say that on some occasions God did kindle acceptable sacrifices. But since there is a double object for this verb, namely, Abel and his sacrifice, this translation is unacceptable, for it would set the man on fire as well as the sacrifice!

That Cain's heart was the real problem here and not the content of his offering can be seen from the last part of verse 5: "So Cain became exceedingly angry and his countenance dropped"—literally, "it burned Cain greatly" (or as we would say, "to the core"), and "his face dropped."

God's displeasure with Cain revealed the sad state of affairs in Cain's heart. Instead of moving to rectify his attitude, Cain let it harden into murder. For the moment, however, anger hid itself in Cain's eyes—he avoided looking anyone in the eye. Averting his own gaze, he kept others from seeing (through the eye gate) what was in his heart.

Hermann Gunkel—who unwisely called this story a myth—was truly unjustified in claiming this story taught that God loved shepherds but not farmers. Despite others who have followed Gunkel's lead, there is no proven connection between this narrative and any parallel stories in the Ancient Near East of rivalries between shepherds and farmers.

Sacrifice in the Old Testament is not a "preapproved" way of earning divine credit. The principle behind it remains the same as it does for all acts of service and ritual in the Christian faith today: God always inspects the giver and the worshiper before he inspects the gift, service or worship.

· C H A P T E R 2 ·

Adam
Lived
930 Years

When Adam had lived 130 years,
he had a son in his own likeness,
in his own image; and he named him Seth.
After Seth was born, Adam lived
800 years and had other sons and daughters.
Altogether, Adam lived 930 years, and then he died.
GENESIS 5:3-5

Everyone who reads the list of the ten antediluvians in Genesis 5 and the list of ten postdiluvians in Genesis 11 is immediately struck by the longevity of these patriarchs. How is it possible, we ask, that these people were able to live so long?

Moreover, we are awed by the ages at which they were still able to father children. Noah became a proud father at a mere 500 years (Gen 5:32)!

The question of the possible reconciliation of the results of scientific inquiry and the claims of Scripture could not be more challenging. The claims for the long lives and the ages at which these men were able to sire children is enough to lead to a distrust of the Scriptures almost from the very first chapters of the Bible.

In fact, so notoriously difficult are the problems presented by the genealogies of Genesis 5 and 11 that they have been paraded for centuries as prime examples of chronological impossibilities in the Bible. A resolution for the kinds of issues raised here are found, however, in an understanding of the writer's method.

As far back as April 1890, William Henry Green of the Princeton faculty wrote an epochal article in the journal *Bibliotheca Sacra*. Green pointed to some clear principles used by the writers of Scripture in the construction of genealogies. Those principles include the following:

1. Abridgment is the general rule because the sacred writers did not want to encumber their pages with more names than necessary.

2. Omissions in genealogies are fairly routine. For example, Matthew 1:8 omits three names between Joram and Ozias (Uzziah); namely, Ahaziah (2 Kings 8:25), Joash (2 Kings 12:1) and Amaziah (2 Kings 14:1). In verse 11, Matthew omits Jehoiakim (2 Kings 23:34). In fact, in Matthew 1:1 the whole of two millennia are summed up in two giant steps: "Jesus Christ, the son of David [about 1000 B.C.], the son of Abraham [about 2000 B.C.]."

3. The meaning of *generation* is more than our twenty to thirty years. In Syriac it equals eighty years. Often in the Exodus account a generation is 100 to 120 years.

4. The meanings of *begat, son of, father of,* and even *bore a son* often have special nuances as the context often indicates. To *beget* often means no more than *to become the ancestor of*. To be *the father of* often means being a grandfather, great-grandfather and more. The point is that the next key person was descended from that male named "father" in the text.

The most instructive lesson of all can be gleaned from Kohath's descent into Egypt (Gen 46:6-11) some 430 years (Ex 12:40) before the exodus. Now if Moses (one in the Kohath line) was 80 years old at the time of the Exodus (Ex 7:7), and no gaps (such as are suggested by the above-mentioned principles) are understood (as we believe the evidence above now forces us to concede), then the "grandfather" of Moses had in Moses' lifetime 8,600 descendants. Amazing as that might seem, here is the real shocker: 2,750 of those 8,600 descendants were males between the ages of 30 and 50 (Num 3:19, 27, 28, 34; 4:36)! It is difficult to believe that the writers of Scripture were that naive.

The form that Genesis 5 and 11 use, with few exceptions, is a stereotypic formula giving the age of the patriarch at the birth of his son, the number of years that he lived after the birth of that son, and then the total number of years that he lived until he died. It is the question of the function of these numbers that attracts our attention here.

Since Zilpah is credited with "bearing" *(yalad)* her grandchildren (Gen 46:18) and Bilhah is said to "bear" *(yalad)* her grandchildren as well (Gen 46:25), it is clear that a legitimate usage of these numbers in the genealogies might well mean that B was a distant relative of A. In this case, the age of A is the age at the birth of that (unnamed) child from whom B (eventually) descended.

The ages given for the "father" when the "son" was born must be actual years, as we shall presently see. The conflation takes place not at the point of supplying the actual years at which the father had a child; it is instead at the point where the name of the next VIP is given. To give a personal illustration, let us suppose that my own father had patriarchal powers of generation and that he had fathered four sons, one when he was 100 and the others when he was 120, 140 and 160. (He didn't, you understand, but I want to illustrate how I understand these genealogies to operate.) Let us say that I, who am the oldest of the four sons in our family, was born when my father was 100. But I was not destined to be the next outstanding person in the line; instead, say, it was my son's son, Walter IV. Accordingly, the biblical narrative would have said that my father, Walter, Sr., lived 100 years (when I was born) and he begat Walter IV (my son's son). The years function, then, as an indicator of the fact that the effects of the Fall into sin had not yet affected human generative powers as seriously as they have more recently. The same point, of course, is to be made with regard to human longevity.

In the above illustration, had the next VIP come through one of my brothers' lines of descent in generations to come, the year when X was born would have been given as 120, 140 or 160, depending which of my (also unnamed brothers) was meant in having secured my father's line of descent to that key figure.

The fact that the record wishes to stress, of course, is the sad mortality of men and women as a result of the sin in the Garden of Eden. The repeated litany "and he died" echoes from the pages like the solemn toll of a funeral bell.

Attempts to make the numbers more palatable have been crushed by the internal weight of their own argumentation or from a failure to care for all the data in a single theory. One abortive attempt was to treat the names as names of tribes rather than as names of individuals. This would seem to work until we meet up with Enoch, who was taken to heaven. It hardly seems fair to imply that the whole Enoch tribe was taken to heaven, so we are left with the idea that these really are meant to represent individuals.

Another, equally unsuccessful, rationalization was that the "years" here represented a system of counting months, or something of that sort. In this view, the years would be reduced by a factor of 10 or 12. Accordingly, Adam's total of 930 years could be reduced to the more manageable and believable 93 or 77 years. This theory runs into trouble when Nahor becomes the father

of Terah at 29 years of age in Genesis 11:24. This would mean
that he actually had a child when he was 2.9 or 2.4 years old! In
that case we jump from the pan into the fire. Unfortunately for
this theory, there are no known biblical examples of the word
year meaning anything less than the *solar year* we are accustomed
to in general speech.

We conclude, then, that while *father* and *son* are sometimes used
to mean *ancestor* and *descendant* in Scripture, they continue to have
a very normative meaning as well. But on the matter of years,
there does not appear to be any variation from the *usus loquendi*—
that is, the sense found in common everyday usage.

One more matter may be worth mentioning at this time.
There is the age-old question of where Cain got his wife. If Adam
and Eve were the first and original parents, how was it possible
for Cain to marry a woman when there is no record of any
females having been born?

But that is just the point! There *is* a record of some being born.
Genesis 5:4 carefully states that Adam had *both sons and daughters*.
The answer to the notorious question is that Cain married his
sister. Given the purity of the race at that time, some of the ill
effects of marrying too close to one's bloodline apparently were
not evident. Furthermore, the proscription against marrying
one's close relatives did not come until the Mosaic legislation in
Leviticus 18.

One final warning might be in order: do not add up the years
of these patriarchs in Genesis 5 and 11 and expect to come up
with the Bible's date for the birth of the human race. The reason
for this warning is clear: the Bible never adds up these numbers.
It is not as though the Bible never gave us a sum of years—there
are the 430 years of Egyptian bondage in Exodus 12:40 and the
480 years of 1 Kings 6:1. But in Genesis 5 and 11 the writer does
not employ his numbers for this purpose; neither should we.

Some who have violated this simple observation have seriously argued that the human race was created on October 24, 4004 B.C., at 9:30 A.M., 45th Meridian time. Being careful scholars from Cambridge, the cynic William Brewster quipped, they did not dare say with any more precision when humankind was born!

The text itself contains a built-in warning not to add up these numbers. Take, for example, the last in this series of patriarchs, Terah (Gen 11:26). It would appear that on his seventieth birthday he had triplets, one of whom was Abram. All of Terah's days were 205 years, according to Genesis 11:32.

There is a problem: Genesis 12:4 implies (and Acts 7:4 affirms) that Abram left Haran after his father died, at which time Abram was only 75 years of age. If Abram was born on his father's seventieth birthday and he was 75 when his father died, 70 plus 75 does not equal the 205 years that are claimed for Terah's life in Genesis 11:32. (It will become clear that Abram was actually born in his father's 135th year. The figure 70 indicates when Terah *began* having the sons listed here.)

Thus those who would have used these genealogies for the purpose of calculating the age of the human race on the earth would have made an error of 60 years at this lower end of the genealogical tables. While this is a small error when placed against the years usually claimed for human antiquity, it still illustrates how wrong-headed this use of the numbers can be.

The last definite date we can fix for any biblical person is around 2100 B.C., for the birth of Abram. The Julian calendar dates for anything before that are impossible to set with the present sets of data at our disposal.

The creation of the universe is dated in Genesis 1:1 as being "in the beginning." Of that we can be as certain as we are of revelation itself. The creation of Adam came six "days" later, but one must be warned that right there in the first chapters of Genesis the Bible uses the word *day* for three different meanings:

(1) daylight (Gen 1:5), (2) a twenty-four-hour day (Gen 1:14) and (3) an epoch or era, as we use the word in speaking of the "day" of the horse and buggy or Abraham Lincoln's "day" (Gen 2:4). I would opt for the day-age theory, given all that must take place on the sixth "day" according to the Genesis record. Incidentally, this day-age view has been the majority view of the church since the fourth century, mainly through the influence of St. Augustine.

So Adam did live a real 930 years. The sons attributed to him may have been his direct sons or they may have been from two to six generations away, but in the same line.

· CHAPTER 3 ·

Enoch Walked with God; Then God Took Him

Altogether, Enoch lived 365 years.
Enoch walked with God;
then he was no more,
because God took him away.
GENESIS 5:23-24

Too many people assume that there is no uniform and sure doctrine on the subject of life after death in the Old Testament. Only one reference in the Old Testament is counted as a clear and undisputed reference to the resurrection of the dead by most Old Testament scholars—Daniel 12:2: "Multitudes who sleep in the dust of the earth will awake: some to everlasting life, others to shame and everlasting contempt." Unhappily, however, even those who concede this point incorrectly place Daniel in the second century B.C.

A few scholars are willing to add Isaiah 26:19 to the Daniel

12:2 passage and count it as a second passage supporting the idea of resurrection of the dead in the Old Testament. It reads: "But your dead will live; their bodies will rise. You who dwell in the dust, wake up and shout for joy. Your dew is like the dew of the morning; the earth will give birth to her dead."

Surely, Isaiah 26:19 ought to count for this doctrine. Nevertheless, it is amazing to see how many learned men and women will deny even these two texts and argue that the Old Testament teaches virtually nothing about resurrection or life after death.

The truth of the matter is that ancient peoples were more attuned to the subject of life after death than moderns suspect. The peoples of the ancient Near East wrote at length about what life was like after one left this earth. One need only consult such representative pieces as the Gilgamesh Epic, The Descent of Ishtar into the Netherworld, the Book of the Dead, and the Pyramid Texts. Indeed, the whole economy of Egypt was geared to the cult of the dead, for all who wished a part in the next life had to be buried around the pyramid of the pharaoh. What these Egyptians could expect in that afterlife was depicted in the scenes on the walls of the Egyptian mortuaries: eating, drinking, singing and all the joys of this life. Each joy, of course, would be magnified and still enjoyed through a body.

By the time Abraham arrived in Egypt, such concepts had been emblazoned on their walls in hieroglyphics, murals and stand-in models made of clay, to make sure no one missed the point. Life after death was not a modern doctrine developed by an educated society that began to think more abstractly about itself and its times. Instead, it was an ancient hunger that existed in the hearts of humanity long before the patriarchs, prophets and kings of the Old Testament began to function. Why should we attribute this idea to the second and third centuries B.C. if already in the third and second *millennium* B.C. there was strong evidence to support it?

The earliest biblical mention of the possibility of a mortal's inhabiting the immortal realms of deity can be found in Genesis 5:24. There we are told that a man named Enoch lived 365 years, all the while "walking with God." Suddenly, "he was not, for God took him."

Enoch, whose name means "beginner," must have been unusually godly—not that he achieved this distinction by removing himself from the world and contemplating only the presence of God. In fact, he fathered the famous Methuselah (the man who lived the longest that we know about on planet earth, 969 years!). And he had other sons and daughters. This man was hardly removed from the daily grind and the problems of life. Nevertheless, he was able to walk with God.

Since this quality of "walking with God" is ascribed only to Enoch and Noah (Gen 6:9), it is significant that Malachi 2:6 shows that the concept involved having a most intimate communion with God. What a tribute to a mortal who is also a sinner! On the other hand, since Exodus 33:20 teaches that "no one may see [God] and live," the possibility of an outward, physical meeting with God is ruled out.

Many think that only since New Testament times have such nearness and inner communion with God become possible. But here was one who found such uninterrupted consciousness of the Living God that it appears to match what we in the post-New Testament era experience.

After 365 years of intimacy with the Almighty, suddenly the Lord "took" Enoch. What can it mean that he "took" him?

The Hebrew root for the verb *to take* is used over a thousand times in the Old Testament. However, in two contexts—this Genesis 5 passage and the account of Elijah's assumption into heaven in 2 Kings 2:3, 10-11—it refers to a snatching of a person's body up to heaven.

In light of these two cases of physical assumption, are there other cases where the verb is used in the Old Testament with a similar meaning?

There are two additional contexts in which more is intended than a mere rescue from dying or distress. Psalm 49 presents a stark contrast between the end of the lives of the wicked and the end of the lives of the righteous. The wicked are like "the beasts that perish" (Ps 49:12, 20) without any hope that they "should live on forever" (v. 9). However, the righteous have the triumphant expectation that "God will redeem [them] from the grave [Hebrew *Sheol*]; he will surely take [them] to himself" (v. 15). The idea is the same as that of Genesis 5:24: God will snatch, take or receive us to himself when we die. If the psalmist had in mind the fact that he would be rescued from death for a few years, though he knows he still must eventually die like the beasts, then the psalm has very little, or no, point.

Psalm 73:23-25 makes a similar contrast between the wicked and the righteous. Once again there is faith that reaches beyond this life, and it centers on this verb *to take* [Hebrew *laqah*]. Says the psalmist, "You guide me with your counsel, and afterward you will take me into glory" (v. 24).

Accordingly, we are on very strong linguistic and conceptual grounds to argue that the "taking" of a person from this earth implies that mortals are capable of inhabiting immortal realms. For the believer in Yahweh in Old Testament times, death did not end it all. There was life after death, and that life was to be in the presence of the Living God.

While Enoch did not experience "resurrection," he did experience glorification. He did, along with Elijah, transcend this mortal life and go in his body to be with God. Since Enoch had not died, he could not be resurrected.

Such a view of an immediate access into the presence of God would also close down all speculation on any kind of intermediate state, receptacle or location as being unscriptural. To say that

Old Testament believers stayed in a separate compartment in Sheol or in a kind of purgatory runs directly counter to the fact that God snatched Enoch and Elijah away *to himself*.

To say that the Old Testament offers the hope of personal fellowship with God beyond the grave with a real body is not outlandish or incorrect. That hope is a teaching of the text itself.

The Sons of God Married the Daughters of Men

When men began to increase in number on the earth
and daughters were born to them, the sons of God saw
that the daughters of men were beautiful,
and they married any of them they chose. Then the Lord said,
"My Spirit will not contend with man forever,
for he is mortal; his days will be a hundred and twenty years."
The Nephilim were on the earth in those days—
and also afterward—when the sons of God
went to the daughters of men and had children by them.
They were the heroes of old, men of renown.
GENESIS 6:1-4

F*ew texts in the history of interpretation have aroused more curiosity and* divergence of opinion than Genesis 6:1-4 has. It is at once tantalizing and deeply puzzling.

What is most difficult is the identification of the main participants in this short narrative—the "sons of God," the "daughters of men" and the "Nephilim" (or "giants") that are mentioned here. An impressive array of scholars has lined up for each of the three major positions taken on the identification of these three groups of participants in the narrative of Genesis 6:1-4. The three positions may be labeled "the cosmologically mixed races view" (angels and humans), "the religiously mixed races view" (godly Sethites and worldly Cainites) and "the sociologically mixed races view" (despotic male aristocrats and beautiful, but common-folk, women).

By all odds, the view that may perhaps claim the greatest antiquity is the cosmologically mixed races, or the angel-theory, view. The pseudepigraphal and noncanonical 1 Enoch, dating from around 200 B.C., claims in 6:1—7:6 that two hundred angels in heaven, under the leadership of Semayaz, noticed that the humans had unusually beautiful and handsome daughters. These they desired for themselves, so they took a mutual oath to go down to earth together, and each took a wife. They taught these wives magical medicine, incantations, the cutting of roots and the care of plants. When the women became pregnant, they gave birth to giants that reached three hundred cubits. The giants in turn consumed all the food, thereby arousing the deep hatred of the earthlings. The giants turned to devouring the people along with the birds, wild beasts, reptiles and fish. Then it was that the earth, having had enough of these huge bullies, brought an accusation against them.

The famous Jewish historian Josephus (born 37 B.C.) also appears to follow this angel theory. He wrote, "Many angels accompanied with women, and begat sons that proved unjust" (*Antiquities* 1.3.1). Likewise, the Greek translation of the Bible of the third century B.C. reads "angels of God" for the phrase "sons of God" in Genesis 6:2. In spite of the antiquity of the cosmologically mixed-races view, there are such overwhelming problems with it that it is not recommended as the solution to this problem. While it is true, of course, that the term "sons of God" does occur in Job 1:6, 2:1 and 38:7 with the meaning "angels" (and that the phrase "sons of the mighty" appears in Ps 29:1 and 89:7 with the meaning "angels"), it cannot fit here for several reasons.

Nowhere else in Scripture are we told that angels married humans. In fact, our Lord specifically stated that angels do not marry (Mt 22:30; Mk 12:25; Lk 20:34-36). And though the Septuagint translated the expression as being equivalent to "angels," it is only the Alexandrian manuscript of that Greek text that does so. The critical edition by Alfred Rahlfs does not reflect the angelic interpretation.

Even more serious is the problem of why judgment should fall on the humans and on the earth if the angels of heaven were the cause of the trouble. God should have flooded heaven, not the earth. The culprits came from above; the women seem to have been doing nothing except being beautiful!

Some, however, will appeal to the New Testament passages of 1 Peter 3:18-20, 2 Peter 2:4 and Jude 6-7 for further support of the angel theory. These passages do not, as a matter of fact, say anything about angelic marriages. To argue from the phrase "in a similar way," of Jude 7, that the sin of Sodom and Gomorrah is the same as the sin of Genesis 6:1-4 claims too much, for the sin of sodomy is not the same thing as marrying a wife from another part of the universe! In fact, "in a similar way" does not compare the sin of the angels with the sin of the men of Sodom and Gomorrah; instead, it compares the sin of Sodom and Gomorrah with the sins of "the cities about them" (that is, Admah and Zeboiim; see Deut 29:23 and Hos 11:8). Thus the sins of Jude's angels (v. 6) and the sins of the five cities of the plain (v. 7) are held up as warnings of the judgment that could come to others. The fall of the angels that Jude mentions is that which took place when Lucifer fell. To connect this fall with the time of the flood because of the proximity of the references in Jude 4-7 would demand that we connect the flood with the overthrow of the five cities of the plain. But the events listed in Jude are successive, not simultaneous: (1) the fall in eternity of Satan (v. 4), (2) the preaching of Noah prior to the flood (v. 5) and (3) the overthrow of Sodom and Gomorrah (v. 6).

To allege that "giants" were the results of such sexual unions is once again to go beyond any data we possess in Scripture. Did the angels procreate without the use of natural bodies? Or did they already possess natural bodies? Or did they create for themselves natural bodies by the use of some mysterious, intrinsic, but rebellious power? Any and all answers to such questions would be purely speculative. To use extracanonical evidence such as 1 Enoch as a witness against or even for Scripture would be unprecedented.

The religiously mixed races view identifies the "sons of God" as the godly line of Seth. Given the sin they committed, they are generally looked on as the apostate line of Seth. "The daughters of men" are equated with the ungodly line of Cain. The sin condemned, then, would be the sin of being "unequally yoked"— that is, that unbelievers should court and marry believers.

This view also fails to meet the test of consistency with the biblical data and context. It uses the term *men* in verses 1 and 2 in two different senses: in verse 1 *men* is used to indicate humanity generically, while in verse 2 *men* is understood suddenly to refer to the Cainite line specifically. Suggesting such an abrupt change in meaning without any indication in the text is unwarranted.

But even more alarming is the problem of the offspring. Why would religiously mixed marriages produce *Nephilim-Gibborim* (or, as some translate this Hebrew expression, "giants")? Does the mixture of pagan and godly genes assure that the offspring's DNA will be wild and grotesque?

This religiously mixed view should be abandoned as well as the cosmologically mixed view. Neither one can stand the weight of the evidence of the passage.

The preferable interpretation of this passage is the sociologically mixed view. "Sons of God" is an early, but typical, reference to the titularies for kings, nobles and aristocrats in the ancient Near Eastern setting. These power-hungry despots not only lusted after power but also were powerfully driven to become "men of a name" (or "men of renown"—v. 4).

In their thirst for recognition and reputation, they despotically usurped control of the states they governed as if they were accountable to no one but themselves. Thus they perverted the whole concept of the state and the provision that God had made for some immediate amelioration of earth's injustices and inequities (Gen 6:5-6; see also Gen 10:8-12). They also became polygamous as they took and married "any of [the women] they chose" (v. 2).

What evidence can be produced for the correctness of this view? There are five lines of evidence. (1) The ancient Aramaic Targums renders "sons of God" as "sons of nobles" (Targums of Onkelos) along with the Greek translation of Symmachus, which reads "the sons of the kings or lords." (2) The word *gods* (Hebrew *Elohim)* is used in Scripture for men who served as magistrates or judges ("Then his master must take him before the judges [*Elohim*]," Ex 21:6; see also Ex 22:8; Ps 82:1, 6). (3) Structurally, the account of the Cainite Lamech (Gen 4:19-24) and that of the "sons of God" in Genesis 6:1-4 are very much alike. In each there is the taking of wives, the bearing of children and the dynastic exploits. The former passage ends with a boast of judgment by Lamech, and the other ends with God's decree of judgment. Lamech practiced bigamy (Gen 4:19), and he enforced his policies by using tyranny. The portraits are parallel and depict states of tyranny, corruption and polygamy. (4) Near Eastern discoveries have validated the pagan use of all sorts of gods' and goddesses' names in order to give more clout and prestige to the governments of Egypt and Mesopotamia—hence the title "sons of God."

The fifth and final line of evidence, concerns the *Nephilim-Gibborim* of Genesis 6:4. The word *Nephilim* occurs only here and in Numbers 13:33, where it refers to the Anakim, who were people of great stature. The root meaning of the word *Nephilim* is "to fall." However, in Genesis 6:4 the word is not just *Nephilim* as in Numbers 13:33; it is *Nephilim-Gibborim*. The word *gibborim* comes from *gibbor*, meaning "a mighty man of valor, strength, wealth, or power." Nimrod, in Genesis 10:8, was such a *gibbor*. He also was clearly a king in the land of Shinar. Hence the meaning of *Nephilim-Gibborim* is not "giants," but something more like "princes," "aristocrats" or "great men."

Genesis 6:1-4 is not depicting the descent of angels to the earth to woo unsuspecting beautiful human women, nor is it a case of the ungodly chasing after pious women of the faith. Instead, it is a case of ambitious, despotic and autocratic rulers seizing both women and power in an attempt to gain all the authority and notoriety they could from those within their reach. Their progeny were, not surprisingly, adversely affected, and so it was that God was grieved over the increased wickedness on planet earth. Every inclination of the hearts and thoughts of humanity was evil. Thus the flood had to come to judge humankind for the perversion of authority, the state, justice and human sexuality.

· CHAPTER 5 ·

God Was Sorry He Had Ever Made Humans

The LORD was grieved that he had made man on the earth, and his heart was filled with pain.
GENESIS 6:6

In Malachi 3:6 God affirms, "I the LORD do not change." This is why Christian doctrine teaches that God is immutable—that is, unchangeable. The promise of this constancy and permanence in the nature and character of God has been deeply reassuring to many believers down through the ages. When everything else changes, we can remember the Living God never fails or vacillates from anything that he is or that he has promised.

For this reason many are legitimately startled when they read that the Lord "was grieved" or "repented" that he had ever made man and woman upon the earth (Gen 6:6). How can both the immutability and the changeableness of God be taught in the same canon of Scripture?

Scriptures frequently use the phrase "God repented." For example, Exodus 32:14 says, "Then [after Moses's intercession for the Israelites] the LORD *relented* and did not bring on his people the disaster he had threatened." Or again in 1 Samuel 15:11, "I am *grieved* that I have made Saul king, because he has turned away from me and has not carried out my instructions." Again in Jeremiah 26:3, "Perhaps they will listen and each will turn from his evil way. Then I will *relent* and not bring on them the disaster I was planning because of the evil they have done." (See also Jer 26:13, 19; Jon 3:10.)

The Hebrew root behind all the words variously translated as "relent," "repent," "be sorry" and "grieve" is the word *naham*. In its origins, the root may well have reflected the idea of breathing, or sighing, deeply. It suggests a physical display of one's feelings—sorrow, compassion or comfort. The root is reflected in such proper names as Nehemiah, Nahum and Menehem.

When God's repentance is mentioned, the point is not that he has changed in his character or in what he stands for. Instead, what we have is a human term being used to refer—rather inadequately—to a perfectly good and necessary divine action. Such a term is called an *anthropomorphism*.

When the Bible says that God repented, the idea is that his feelings toward some person or group of persons changed in response to some change on the part of the objects of his action or some mediator who intervened (often by God's own direction and plan). Often in the very same passages that announce God's repentance, there is a firm denial of any alteration in God's plan, purpose or character. Thus 1 Samuel 15:29 reminds us that "he who is the Glory of Israel does not lie or change his mind; for he is not a man, that he should change his mind." Yet Samuel made that statement the day after the Lord told him that he was *grieved* he had made Saul king (1 Sam 15:11).

From our human perspective, then, it appears that the use of this word indicates that God indeed changed his purpose. But the expression "to repent," when used of God, is anthropopathic (that is, a description of our Lord in terms of human emotions and passions).

In Genesis 6:6, the repentance of God is his proper reaction to continued and unrequited sin and evil in the world. The parallel clause says that sin filled his heart with pain. This denotes no change in his purpose or character. It only demonstrates that God has emotions and passions and that he can and does respond to us for good or ill when we deserve it.

The point is that unchangeableness must not be thought of as if it were some type of frozen immobility. God is not some impervious being who cannot respond when circumstances or individuals change. Rather, he is a living person, and as such he can and does change when the occasion demands it. He does not change in his character, person or plan. But he can and does respond to our changes.

· C H A P T E R 6 ·

Noah Was a Righteous and Blameless Man

Noah was a righteous man,
blameless among the people of his time,
and he walked with God.
GENESIS 6:9

Genesis 6:9 is a hard saying because it appears to imply that Noah attained moral and spiritual perfection. How could Noah have achieved such an elevated status of perfection when he came after the the Fall of Adam and Eve in the garden? Did he not partake of the sinful nature and the bent toward depravity that all the race had inherited? If he did, as most will affirm, in what sense could it be said that he was "righteous" and "blameless"?

Noah, Daniel and Job are remembered for their righteous lives (Ezek 14:14, 20). But they did not as humans set the standard for others. The standard they shared is still the same today: it is the Lord himself who sets the standard. His nature and will compose the ethical and moral measuring stick for all others to follow.

The Hebrew word *saddiq* (which shares the same root as the Hebrew word *sedeq)* basically connotes conformity to the standard. The original idea may well have been "to be straight." From this came the idea of a "norm," and of being "in the right." The bureau of standards for what was morally and ethically right was to be found only in God himself. "The Lord is righteous [*saddiq*] in all his ways and loving toward all he has made" (Ps 145:17). Therefore, the standards and judgments set out in his Word are righteous (Ps 119:144, 160, 172).

Some of the earlier usages of the word occur in connection with the Israelite judges' carrying out of their functions and decisions. They were warned: "Do not pervert justice; do not show partiality to the poor or favoritism to the great, but judge your neighbor *fairly" (sedeq*—Lev 19:15). This same type of "righteousness" applied to scales and weights: "Use *honest [sedeq]* scales and *honest* weights, an *honest* ephah and an *honest* hin" (Lev 19:36). Thus, the righteousness of God opposed commercial or judicial fraud and deception.

Righteousness applies to three areas of personal relationships: the ethical, the forensic and the theological. None of these three areas depended on current norms or practices; the righteousness that God wanted could be found only in the standards set forth in his Word. The ethical area dealt with the conduct of persons with one another. The forensic aspect required equality before the law for all (small and great, rich and poor). The theological aspect demanded that God's covenant people live a life of holiness, following the path laid out by God's righteousness.

In the case of Noah, he conformed to the standard set by God. When all the people around him were immersing themselves in evil and earning the deep wrath and judgment of God, Noah bucked the trend and set his heart to follow the path found in the person and character of God. He stood his ground and remained uninfluenced by all that was happening around him.

The word *righteous* simply meant that he accepted and used the righteous standard for his living and acting. It does not imply perfection. The term does not in itself establish total approbation of his actions, any more than it does in connection with Tamar in Genesis 38:26. The text expresses an estimate of the comparative rightness of Tamar and Judah. When Judah was exposed as the adulterer by whom Tamar had become pregnant, he said, "She is more righteous than I"—that is, she was more within her rights to act as she did than Judah was in what he did. This can hardly be a complete endorsement of Tamar or her actions. Neither is the use of the same term a total endorsement of Noah.

Noah met the basic requirement set by the norm God had erected, and his conduct proved it. This can also be seen from the parallel clause "and he walked with God"—the same wording that was used of Enoch (Gen 5:24).

But this still leaves the problem of Noah's being called "blameless," or "perfect." Scripture has one preeminent example of the "perfect" man: Job. It is said that he was "blameless" (that is, "perfect"—Job 1:1). He too claimed that he was "blameless" or "perfect" in Job 9:21-22; 12:4; and 31:6. Even under heavy assault to the contrary, he held fast to his "integrity" (same root—Job 27:5). And he was not alone in this opinion, for his wife ascribed "integrity" to him (Job 2:9). Surprisingly enough, Yahweh in heaven agreed that Job was indeed "blameless" or "perfect" (Job 1:8; 2:3).

In spite of all these high accolades for Job, he knew that he was a sinner, for he queried, "How can a mortal be righteous before God?" (Job 9:2). He further acknowledged his sin (Job 10:6; 14:16-17). Accordingly, the use of the word *blameless* or *perfect* does not imply that one has attained perfection or a state in which one no longer sins. Even the creature in Eden (probably Lucifer) that was created "perfect" was found to be capable of sin (Ezek 28:13-15).

The Hebrew root of the word *perfect* involves the idea of completeness. Thus we conclude that Noah conformed to the standard set by God, and that his life was "complete" and well rounded out, with no essential quality missing.

The modifying phrase "among the people of his time" indicates all the more clearly that Noah's righteousness and blamelessness stood out against his contemporaries' sinfulness.

Just as Job had to admit his sin, so the same Scripture that tells us that Noah was righteous and blameless also tells us that he became drunk from the fruit of the vine (Gen 9:21). Clearly, there is no case for perfection and sinlessness in these words *righteous* and *blameless*. Instead, there is a case for someone who walked with God and delighted in following what he had said and living by the standards he had established.

· CHAPTER 7 ·

Noah Brought Two (or Seven) of Each Kind

*You are to bring into the ark two of all living creatures,
male and female, to keep them alive with you. Two of every kind
of bird, of every kind of animal and of every kind of creature
that moves along the ground will come to you to be kept alive. . . .
Take with you seven of every kind of clean animal, a male and its mate,
and two of every kind of unclean animal, a male and its mate,
and also seven of every kind of bird, male and female,
to keep their various kinds alive throughout the earth.*
GENESIS 6:19-20; 7:2-3

During the last century and a half, the prevailing nonevangelical interpretation of the Noah story taught in university religion classes, and now in many churches, is that this is not one story but at least two separate stories poorly patched together in an attempt to make them one unified whole. Evidence offered for the existence of two original stories is the fact that Noah is first told to take two of each kind of animal on board the ark and then to take seven of each clean kind.

In the final analysis, according to one eminent critical scholar, there is only one piece of evidence for the disunity of the Noah story, and that is repetition or repeated occurrence. The repetition, he reasoned, makes no sense unless two or more narratives have been conflated.

Repetition *can* sometimes be a sign of divergent traditions and of a later editor's having welded together several versions of the same story, or even different stories. But there are other explanations for this same phenomenon. Repetition is one of the most fundamental tools of the literary artist. Its presence does not necessarily indicate that the literary piece is a composite hodge-podge reflecting heterogeneous elements of mixed sources, oral or written.

To claim, as many have done, that 6:19-20 came from a priestly source around 450 B.C. and that 7:2-3 came from an earlier Yahwistic source around 850 B.C. is to say that the editor of the material let the contradiction stand. There is no need for such extravagant theories of origins, especially since we have a second-millennium flood story from Mesopotamia, the Gilgamesh Epic, with many of the same details. The Gilgamesh Epic, only unearthed in this century, could hardly have incorporated the so-called priestly and Yahwistic sources from the fifth and ninth centuries B.C., having been written and buried long before then. Why then must we suppose that Genesis incorporates such allegedly later sources?

The truth is that there is no inherent incompatibility between the two texts as they presently stand. Genesis 7:2-3 is just more precise than 6:19-20 on the question of the types and numbers of animals and birds that would board the ark.

Noah's first instruction was to admit pairs of all kinds of creatures on the ark to preserve their lives (6:19-20). That was the basic formula. Then he was given more specific instructions about admitting seven pairs of each of the clean animals and seven pairs of each kind of bird. The purpose of this measure was to become clear only after the flood. Birds would be needed to reconnoiter the earth (8:7-12), and the clean animals and birds would be offered in sacrifice to the Lord (8:20). If Noah had taken only one pair of each and then offered each of these pairs in sacrifice, these species would have become completely extinct.

The simplest and most adequate explanation is that chapter 6 of Genesis contains general summary directions—take two of each. After Noah had understood these general instructions, God spoke more specifically about the role the clean beasts and birds were to play.

Scripture does not indicate how the distinction between "clean" and "unclean" arose. Later on the Mosaic law would sanction this distinction and formally define it. But we are left without any indication of the origin of the distinction, just as we are left in the dark regarding how and when the whole idea of sacrifice started. Cain and Abel both sacrificed, but a formal declaration inaugurating this ritual is not recorded.

If some analysts still gamely wish to excise the clean animals from the so-called priestly account of the Genesis flood story, they only introduce into what they are calling the Yahwistic account the very sort of repetition that they had earlier taken as a sign of divergent sources. This is too high a price to pay just to avoid admitting that perhaps the accounts of the boarding of pairs of unclean animals are connected with the boarding of seven pairs of clean animals. Genesis 7:6-15 does not support a Yahwistic-and-priestly-source explanation; indeed, it causes unusual trouble for such an analysis of the material. To split the clean from the unclean animals in this story is not a Solomonic move, for even Solomon did not split the baby. Neither should we.

· C H A P T E R 8 ·

Cursed
Be
Canaan

When Noah awoke from his wine and found out
what his youngest son [Ham] had done to him,
he said, "Cursed be Canaan! The lowest
of slaves will he be to his brothers."
GENESIS 9:24-25

O*ne of the saddest moments in the history of interpretation was when*
advocates of slavery decided to use this text as a justification for
their less-than-human treatment of dark-skinned people. All too
easily it was assumed that this divine prophecy given by Noah
after the flood legitimized slavery for a group of people who had
been cursed perpetually. Supporters of slavery argued that the
Arabic version of Genesis 9:25 reads "Cursed be the father of
Canaan" instead of "Cursed be Canaan." A vehement allegiance
to the misapplication of this text has continued among some
groups to the present day. The oppression of blacks by whites
cannot be justified from this story about Noah's wine-drinking.

Noah, the righteous and blameless man, had been drinking wine (Gen 9:21). That in itself was not the issue here, for in Scripture wine is viewed as one of God's gifts to humankind (Ps 104:15). Every burnt and peace offering was accompanied by a libation of wine (Num 15:5-10), and the drinking of wine at festivals was acknowledged (Deut 14:26). One of the symbols for Israel was the vine (Is 5:1-7; Mk 12:1-11).

But the Bible also warns about the dangers of wine. Nazirites were to abstain from all alcohol and wine (Num 6:3-4), and priests were forbidden to drink prior to officiating in the sanctuary lest they die (Lev 10:9). The laity were also warned that drinking too much wine was dangerous to people and offensive to God (Prov 21:17; 23:20-21, 29-35; Is 5:22).

Drunkenness was especially reprehensible when it led to self-exposure (Hab 2:15; Lam 4:21). The exposure of one's nakedness was not only publicly demeaning but also incompatible with the presence of the living God (Ex 20:26; Deut 23:12-14).

Because Noah drank to excess, he became drunk. The heat generated by the alcohol in his bloodstream led the patriarch to thrust off his covering involuntarily as he lay in his tent. The reflexive form of the verb makes it clear that he uncovered himself (Gen 9:21).

Noah's youngest son, Ham, entered the tent, and there he was confronted with the situation we have just described (9:22). Apparently his gaze was not a mere harmless notice or an accidental glance. The verb used here has such force that some say it means "he gazed with satisfaction."

What exactly Ham did has been the subject of much speculation. The most bizarre of all suggestions is that Ham castrated his father Noah in a struggle for family power. But there is no evidence to support this idea other than the precedent of some Greek and Semitic stories with the motif of paternal castration. A second suggestion is that the expression "to see a man's nakedness" is an idiomatic phrase for sexual intercourse with that man's wife. But this expression is quite different from the idiom "to uncover the nakedness" of Leviticus 18 and 20. Leviticus 20:17 is the only place where the verb "to see" is used, but it is not in a parallel construction with "uncover." The view that Ham had an incestuous relationship with his mother is an impossible explanation. Even if Ham had committed incest with his mother, he would hardly have told his brothers!

Thus, Ham could be faulted simply for this: he failed to cover up his father's nakedness and chose rather to make fun of his father to his brothers. Such an act was serious enough to prompt Noah to utter his curse on Ham's descendants, who would be guilty of the kinds of sexual perversions that many suspected Ham of carrying out. To lie exposed meant that one was unprotected, dishonored and at risk of exploitation. Ham had transgressed a natural and sacred barrier. His disgusting ridicule of his father before his brothers aggravated the act and perhaps betrayed a moral weakness that had established itself in his personality.

Who, then, was Canaan? And why was he cursed if Ham was the culprit? Since the Law of God insists that God deals with all people justly, this curse of Canaan is all the more puzzling.

Genesis 10:6 lists the sons of Ham as Cush (basically Ethiopia), Mizraim (Egypt), Put (generally taken to be one of the North African countries) and Canaan (of the country of Palestine/Canaan). We are not talking about Africans or blacks here, but the Canaanite peoples who inhabited ancient Palestine.

Canaan was not singled out for the curse because he was the youngest son of Ham, nor was it a random selection. Apparently, Noah saw in the youngest son of Ham the same tendencies and perversions that had been evidenced in Ham. When Noah had fully recovered from the effects of his drunkenness, he uttered this curse against Canaan. Noah could not have cursed his son

Ham, for he and his brothers, along with Noah, had been the objects of a blessing in Genesis 9:1. Neither Noah nor anyone else could reverse such a blessing with a curse. Balaam the son of Beor learned this the hard way in Numbers 22—24.

Still, there may well have been an element of "mirroring" punishment here, especially if Canaan was to exhibit the outworkings of the tendencies already present in Ham's failure to cover Noah's nakedness. Finally, it is a matter of historical record that the Canaanites were notoriously deviant in their sexual behavior. Almost everywhere the archaeologist's spade has dug in that part of the world, there have been fertility symbols accompanying texts explicit enough to make many a modern pornographic dealer seem a mere beginner in the trade of deviant sexuality. Sodom left its name for the vice these people practiced. Even the Romans, so depraved in their own practices, were shocked by the behavior of the Phoenicians at the colony of Carthage (the last vestige of the Canaanite race).

The curse was on Canaan. So abject was the servitude to which Canaan was subjected that the superlative genitive, "servant of servants," implied that his condition would pass on to future generations.

Why, then, was this story included in the biblical narrative? It tells the reader that unless there was some moral change in the Canaanites, they were slated for removal from their land. That God is long-suffering and slow to anger is attested by the fact that this judgment did not fall on that group of descendants until the time of Joshua's conquest of Canaan. It is impossible to date Noah's times, but it's known that Joshua lived around 1400 B.C. At a minimum this would mean that the grace of God was extended to the Canaanites for several millennia. Surely God was most generous with these people, giving more than adequate time for sinners to repent.

· CHAPTER 9 ·

Abraham Said of Sarah, "She Is My Sister"

As [Abram] was about to enter Egypt, he said to his wife Sarai,
"I know what a beautiful woman you are. When the Egyptians see you,
they will say, 'This is his wife.' Then they will kill me but will let you live.
Say you are my sister, so that I will be treated well for your sake
and my life will be spared because of you."
GENESIS 12:11-13

For a while he stayed in Gerar, and there Abraham said of his wife Sarah,
"She is my sister." Then Abimelech king of Gerar sent for Sarah and took her.
But God came to Abimelech in a dream one night and said to him,
"You are as good as dead because of the woman you have taken;
she is a married woman."
GENESIS 20:1-3

These two passages, along with a third about Isaac in Genesis 26:6-11, have the same theme of the wife being passed off as a sister. In all three episodes the plot is essentially the same. A patriarch visits a foreign land, accompanied by his wife. Fearing that his wife's beauty will become a source of danger to himself, he resorts to the subterfuge of pretending that his wife is his sister.

The recurrent wife-sister theme in Genesis has provoked an unusual number of comments and speculative solutions. Interpreters have been puzzled about why father and son should have fallen back on this ploy so frequently.

The old explanation, the documentary source hypothesis, was that there was a single story told in different parts of the country at different times with different heroes. When these various traditions were welded together, the rough edges of the original sources were left for more intelligent moderns to detect. Hence Genesis 12:10-20 came from the Yahwistic writer of the "J" document, offering a Judean or southern viewpoint, and a written source coming from around 850 B.C. The Isaac parallel likewise came from the "J" document, but it featured another protagonist, Isaac. Genesis 20:1-18 was attributed to the "E" document, since it favored a northern or Ephraimite viewpoint and was committed to writing about a century later than "J"—that is, about 750 B.C.

Even though critical scholars concerned themselves with determining which story was the original and how the others developed from it, there is no compelling reason to doubt that all three incidents occurred. But why did the writer find it necessary to include all three stories? When you have heard a joke once, who wants to hear it again?

Such an attitude betrays a lack of feeling for Hebrew rhetoric, in which repetition was a favorite device. Yet more is at work here. The two protagonists of these stories, Abram—or as he was later renamed, Abraham—and Isaac, were at the center of the promise-plan by which God was going to bless the very nations they were coming in contact with. Moreover, the means by which God was going to bless these gentile nations was to be carried in the womb of the very woman to whom these potentates were being attracted. Each of these stories, then, sets up a moment of real suspense for divine providence and for the pa-

triarchs, who, in spite of all their blundering, lying and misman-
agement, were still the means through which God was going to
bless the world.

It must be stated clearly that Abraham and Isaac both practiced
deception. The Bible merely reports that they did so, without
approving of it. God preserved the purity of Sarah and Rebekah
in spite of all the maneuverings of their husbands. No one can
make a case for lying based on these passages. It will always be
wrong to lie, since God is truth.

What about half-lies? Wasn't it true that Sarah was Abraham's
half-sister? Was it not also true that the Hurrian society, in such
centers as Haran where Abraham had stayed on his way to Canaan, had a special legal fiction in which the bonds of marriage
were strengthened when the groom adopted his wife as his "sister" in a legal document parallel to the marriage contract?

Yes, both are true. Sarah was Abraham's half-sister (Gen
11:29). And there was the Hurrian legal form of sister-marriage.
However, most scholars have now concluded that there is very
little basis for assuming that Abraham had such a document in
mind, since the details of patriarchal and Hurrian marriage documents are quite different.

What, then, was Abraham's motivation? Was he willing to
sacrifice his wife's honor and allow her to marry any suitor in
order to save his own skin and possibly get some financial gain?
Though Genesis 12:13 might appear to support such an interpretation, subsequent events (vv. 15-16) provide a basis for ques-
tioning its correctness. Oriental attitudes toward adultery were
much more sensitive than ours (Gen 20:2-9). It is doubtful that
Abraham would have allowed his wife to bear that sin on her
conscience, much less allow himself to be an accomplice in such
a sin.

The medieval commentators suggested that what Abraham
hoped to get out of his "brother" status was the right to receive

and deny all suitors' requests to be Sarah's husband. This suggestion works in those stories where brothers attempt to delay their sister's marriage (Laban and Rebekah in Gen 24:55, and Dinah and her brothers in Gen 34:13-17).

Abraham and Isaac are to be condemned for their complicity in lying, no matter how noble a motive they may have had, or how much truth the lie contained. Still, God was not to be deterred in his plan to bring life and blessing to the nations through the offspring of Sarah and Rebekah.

Abraham
Was Gathered
to His People

*Then Abraham breathed his last
and died at a good old age,
an old man and full of years;
and he was gathered to his people.*
GENESIS 25:8

What was the Old Testament saints' concept of life after death? Did they have a clear belief in life after death? If so, what did it involve? For example, was it a ghostly existence? Did it involve personal, conscious awareness? Did they expect the spirit to be joined with a body? At what point? All of these questions are relevant to understanding this text about Abraham.

The expression "to be gathered to one's people" is similar to another expression, "to go to one's fathers," found in Genesis 15:15. The former phrase is found frequently—for example, in Genesis 25:8, 17; 49:29, 33; Deuteronomy 32:50; and 2 Kings 22:20.

Do these phrases simply mean, as many scholars claim, that the Old Testament individual was laid to rest in the family grave? Is it true that there was no thought of an afterlife?

By Abraham's time, the human life span had been so curtailed, due to the physical effects of the Fall in the Garden of Eden, that 175 years was regarded as a "good old age." What happened after Abraham died? Was he simply buried with his ancestors—end of story? Unfortunately, all too many carelessly conclude that this is precisely the case.

Actually, the expression "he was gathered to his people" or "he went to his fathers" cannot mean that he was buried with his relatives and ancestors. In Genesis 25:8-9 such an analysis is impossible, because we know that none of Abraham's kin, except his wife, was buried at the cave of Machpelah.

In the Old Testament, those who have already died are regarded as still existing. The event of being "gathered to one's people" is always distinguished from the act of burial, which is described separately (Gen 25:8-9; 35:29; 49:29, 31, 33). In many cases only one ancestor was in the tomb (1 Kings 11:43; 22:40) or none at all (Deut 31:16; 1 Kings 2:10; 16:28; 2 Kings 21:18), so that being "gathered to one's people" could not mean being laid in the family sepulcher.

Readers of the text should not infer something special from the use of *Sheol* in some of these texts. In every one of the sixty-five instances of *Sheol* in the Old Testament, it refers simply to "the grave," not to the shadowy region of the netherworld. The writer of the book of Hebrews, in the New Testament, supports the notion that the patriarchs expected an afterlife:

> All these people [from Abel to Abraham] were still living by faith when they died. They did not receive the things promised; they only saw them and welcomed them from a distance. And they admitted that they were aliens and strangers on earth. People who say such things show that they are looking

for a country of their own. If they had been thinking of the country they had left, they would have had opportunity to return. Instead, they were longing for a better country—a heavenly one. Therefore God is not ashamed to be called their God, for he has prepared a city for them. (Heb 11:13-16)

Here is a clear testimony that through faith, these early participants in the promises of God were fully expecting to enjoy life after death. While the full revelation of the life hereafter and the resurrection of the body awaited a later unveiling in the Old and New Testaments, the common assertion that the Old Testament saint knew nothing at all about such a possibility is a preconceived error.

In Genesis 17:8 Abraham was given a promise by God: "The whole land of Canaan, where you are now an alien, I will give as an everlasting possession *to you* and your descendants after you." The rabbis reasoned that since Abraham never actually enjoyed the fulfillment of this promise, he would be raised from the dead to possess the land.

While this reasoning is curious, it is not all that far off. It is no more fanciful than the reasoning of our Lord in reminding the Sadducees—who did not believe in the resurrection—that the God of Abraham, Isaac and Jacob was not the God of the dead but of the living. Thus the patriarchs were not to be counted out of the hope of resurrection (Mt 22:23-32). The believer's relationship to God carries with it life in the body now and immortality in the future.

If some object that such concepts are too "developed" for the primitive times and minds of Old Testament people, we need only remind each other that life after death already was the overriding passion of the Egyptian culture. It was to be a life of material things, with real bodies, real wine, women and song. That concept had been imaged in the pyramid monuments for a thousand years before Abraham arrived in Egypt. How, then, could the afterlife be an impossible concept for him?

Other evidences of the belief of a real life after death are afforded by the stern warnings from Mosaic times about any dabbling in necromancy, the cult of contacting the dead. What harm would there have been in fooling around with something that had no reality? Already in the middle of the second millennium B.C., the Israelites knew the afterlife was real, and thus they were warned not to be involved in any contacting of individuals who had passed beyond this world.

Abraham died and was buried. But he also joined a community of believers who had gone on before. No details of the nature of that community are given at this point. But these expressions, "to be gathered to one's people" and "to go to one's fathers," are not a mere euphemism for death without any clear theological import. The evidence argues to the contrary.

Jacob Wrestled with God Until Daybreak

So Jacob was left alone, and a man wrestled
with him till daybreak. . . . Then the man said, "Your
name will no longer be Jacob, but Israel, because you have
struggled with God and with men and have overcome."
GENESIS 32:24, 28

According to Martin Luther, *"Every man holds that this text is one* of the most obscure in the Old Testament." There is probably no commentator who can so expound this experience of Jacob as to clear up every question we could raise about what it was that happened here.

The principal issue is the identity of the man who wrestled with Jacob at the Jabbok ford all night until the dawn of the next day. Was this individual a mere mortal, or was he an angel? Or, still more startling, was this individual actually a preincarnate form of the Son of God, the second person of the Trinity?

Some have attempted to solve the interpretive problem by

making the whole sequence a dream narrative. Josephus understood it as a dream wherein the apparition made use of words and voices *(Antiquities* 1.20.2). Others have been content to allegorize the story, viewing it as the fight of the soul against the passions and vices hidden within oneself (for example, Philo, *Legum Allegoriae* 3.190). Clement of Alexandria did equate the wrestler with the Logos of John's Gospel, but he argues that the Logos remained unknown by name to Jacob because Jesus had not yet appeared in the flesh *(Paedagogus* 1.7.57).

Jewish literature, recognizing that there was an actual fight at the heart of the story, says that the struggle was with the prince or angel of Esau, named Samael, rather than with any theophany, much less a christophany.

Others, like Jerome, have tried to make the episode a portrayal of long and earnest prayer. Such prayer involved meditation on the divine presence, confession of sin and a deep yearning for communication with the divine.

Modern interpreters, chary of assuming any real contact of mortals with the immortal or supernatural, prefer to identify the story with the types of myth that have gods fighting with heroes. Of course this point of view would devalue the narrative into pure fiction and attribute its source not to revelation, but to literary borrowing from other polytheistic mythologies. Such a solution stands condemned under the weight of its own assertions when lined up against the claims of the biblical text itself.

The best commentary ever written on this passage is to be found in Hosea 12:3-4:

> As a man [Jacob] struggled with God. He struggled with the angel and overcame him; he wept and begged for his favor. He found him at Bethel and there [God] talked with *us.* (my translation)

Hosea 12:4 describes the antagonist, then, as an "angel." But since Old Testament appearances of God, or theophanies, are routinely described as involving the "angel of the Lord," it should not surprise us that the Lord of glory took the guise or form of an angel. In fact, that is exactly what God would do later on in his enfleshment, or incarnation. He would take on flesh; in his coming as a babe to Bethlehem, however, he took on human flesh forever.

But what really clinches the argument for this identification is the fact that in verse 3 of Hosea 12, the parallel clause equates this "angel" with God himself. Jacob struggled with an "angel," yes, but he also "struggled with God."

What makes this identification difficult to conceive is the fact that the encounter involved wrestling. How is it possible for the second person of the Trinity—for that is the person connected with the "angel of the Lord" so frequently—to grapple in such a physical way with a mortal?

Clearly there is a sort of punning wordplay in this story with Jacob (ya'aqob), Jabbok (yabboq) and the action of wrestling (ye'abeq). These similar-sounding words attract hearers' and readers' attention to the linking of the story's key ideas. The wrestling took place at the threshold of the Promised Land. Ever since Jacob's flight from his disaffected brother Esau, Jacob had been outside the land God had deeded to him in his promise.

As a result of this wrestling, Jacob was renamed Israel and prepared for his part in fathering the nation that God had promised. In order to preserve Jacob's memory of this spiritual crisis, God left a permanent mark on his body. God touched Jacob's thigh and dislocated it, so that he limped from that point onward.

Unfortunately, we cannot identify the exact nature of the wrestling. It is clear, however, that it involved more than a battle in the spiritual realm. It left Jacob with a real physical impairment. Therefore, while Genesis says that Jacob wrestled with a "man" rather than the Lord's angel, this person told him that he had wrestled "with God" and had "overcome" (Gen 32:28); similarly, Hosea says that he "overcame" an angel (Hos 12:4).

Incidentally, the touch on Jacob's thigh became the basis in postexilic times for a food taboo in the Jewish community. Jews may not eat the sinew of the nerve along the thigh joint, called the *nervus ischiadicus* or sciatic nerve.

We conclude that the "man" or "angel" with whom Jacob wrestled was Jesus himself, in a temporary incarnate form prior to his permanent enfleshment when he would come to earth as a human baby. This is consistent with other places in the Old Testament where the "angel of the Lord" is identified as the second person of the Trinity.

• C H A P T E R 1 2 •

The Scepter
Will Not Depart
Until Shiloh Comes

The scepter will not depart from Judah,
nor the ruler's staff from between his feet,
until he comes to whom it belongs
and the obedience of the nations is his.
GENESIS 49:10

Rarely, *if ever, has one word had as many possible meanings or* emendations attached to it, with no general agreement or consensus being reached, as the word *Shiloh* as it appears in Genesis 49:10. The clause in the NIV rendered "until he comes to whom it belongs" is more literally "until Shiloh comes."

What did the patriarch Jacob have in mind as he spoke his blessing to his fourth son, Judah, and predicted the arrival of "Shiloh"? It is clear from a postexilic text (1 Chron 5:1-2) that Joseph and Judah shared what would have been the blessings normally inherited by the firstborn, Reuben. Joseph received the double portion, and through Judah the line of the "ruler" was to come. This helps us understand the way later generations were taught under inspiration to regard the role Judah played, but what are we to make of Jacob's understanding of the blessing he pronounced on Judah in Genesis 49?

Did Jacob intend to point to a future city where the Ark of the Covenant would rest until that city came to an end? Why then did Jacob speak of *"his* feet" and the obedience that would be *his?* The antecedent of the pronouns seems to be a person, not an object like the city Shiloh.

If Jacob did not intend to point to a city named Shiloh, did he have a specific person in mind? And if he did, did the name mean "Rest" or "Peace-giver?" Or are we to take the alleged Akkadian cognate word and conclude that the name means "Ruler"?

Perhaps this name is only a title meaning something like "His Peace." Or perhaps we are to accept one or another of the numerous emendations (changes in spelling of the Hebrew *Shiloh,* all of which have particular nuances of meaning).

Most startling of all is the statement that someone from the tribe of Judah would own the obedience, not just of the tribe or even of all Israel, but of all the nations. This suggests a kingship that would extend well beyond the boundaries of the ancient land of Israel.

The problem, then, is clear; the solution is more difficult. Let us note first of all that the scepter symbolizes the rule and dominion exercised by a ruler. The "ruler's staff" or "commander's staff" may be a parallel synonym to "scepter." But since its verbal root means to inscribe or to cut, as in setting forth a decree, the term may refer to the concept of a lawgiver, one who proclaims the law or rules and governs on the basis of law. Given the context of Judah as the person in view, it would seem better to take "ruler's staff" as a correlative term with "scepter." It would then mean one who wields the scepter, power and authority on the basis of the decree or law given to him.

Now comes the more difficult phrase, "until Shiloh comes." The "until" is used not in an *exclusive* but an *inclusive* sense. That is, the coming of Shiloh does not mark the limits of Judah's domination over the nation of Israel, for if it did it would constitute a threat and not a blessing. Instead, the idea is that the sovereignty of Judah is brought to its highest point under the arrival and rule of Shiloh.

Who or what, then, is "Shiloh"? It cannot refer to the place where the tabernacle would be pitched centuries later. If it did, Jacob would be prophesying about a place that was unknown at the time of prediction, and one that was rarely if ever mentioned in the literature of later years except as a symbol of judgment. This interpretation would also involve changing the verb "comes" to "come to an end," a meaning that adds more than the text says and only raises another question: what end and why?

Martin Luther connected Shiloh with the Hebrew *shilyah*, "womb." This would suggest the son of the womb of the Messiah. John Calvin had a similar idea. He connected Shiloh with the Hebrew *shil*, plus the third-person suffix, meaning "his son." But Luther and Calvin failed to realize that these were two different words. *Shil* does not mean "son." In modern Hebrew *shil* or *shilil* means "embryo." The closest biblical Hebrew comes to the form Calvin was thinking of is *shilyah*, "afterbirth."

Others have looked for a verbal root rather than a nominal one. One connects it to *shalah*, "to be peaceful"—hence "Rest," or perhaps "Man of Peace." Another suggests the verb *shalal*, "to draw out or plunder," with the pronoun "his"—hence "his drawn-out one," or "his child to be born." One other view connects the word with *shalah*, "to send." This would yield "until he who is sent comes."

Since the second half of the poetic line begins with "and to him" in the emphatic position, it is proper to assume that we are dealing with a coming person. Moreover, since "to him shall be the obedience of the nations," he will be a ruler who will emanate from the line of Judah.

The rabbis were convinced that Ezekiel 21:27 (v. 32 in the Hebrew) provided the proper clue for the meaning of Shiloh. They suggested that behind this word lies *shel*, meaning "which," and *loh*, meaning "belongs to him." Thus understood, the meaning of Shiloh accords with Ezekiel 21:27, "until he comes to whom it rightfully belongs."

Up to the time of Ezekiel, of course, the tribe of Judah had evidenced no leadership that would foreshadow a ruler who would come through Judah's line. All they had done was lead the march through the wilderness (Num 10:14). But when the Israelites got to the promised land, Judah's inheritance had been allotted first (Josh 15:1). Later, Judah would emerge as the leader of the tribes in a totally new way. Thus Jacob referred as much to Judah as he did to the successor who would come through his line.

The verses that follow our passage, Genesis 49:11-12, have a lush rural setting. They describe the rich blessings in store for Judah and this ruling successor, the Messiah himself. There would be great prosperity for the coming royal one, but there would also be pain and bloodshed (perhaps the references to wine and the treading of the winepress imply this struggle).

Shiloh, we conclude, is the royal Messiah who comes through the line of Judah and who will take the throne that rightfully belongs to him.

· C H A P T E R 1 3 ·

The Lord
Was About to
Kill Moses

*At a lodging place on the way, the LORD met Moses
and was about to kill him. But Zipporah took a flint knife,
cut her son's foreskin and touched Moses' feet with it.
"Surely you are a bridegroom of blood to me," she said.
So the LORD let him alone. (At that time she said
"bridegroom of blood," referring to circumcision.)*
EXODUS 4:24-26

What surprises and puzzles us about this text is its brevity, the abruptness of its introduction, the enigmatic nature of its cryptic statements and the difficulty of establishing the correct antecedents for several of its pronouns. But most troubling of all is the bald statement that the Lord wanted to kill the leader he had worked to prepare for eighty years.

These verses are some of the most difficult in the book of Exodus. Why did the Lord wish to kill Moses? What had he done—or failed to do? Why did his Midianite wife, Zipporah, pick up a flint knife without being told to do so and immediately circumcise her son? What is the significance of her taking her son's excised prepuce and touching Moses' feet while complaining, "Surely you are a bridegroom of blood to me"? Why did the Lord then let Moses go? (It would seem that Moses is the one to whom the pronoun "him" refers). All of these problems have made this brief account one of the hard sayings of the Old Testament.

The narrative begins with an adverb meaning "at that time." This immediately solves one problem: this text is not an etiological story (that is, an attempt to explain why certain things function or have the meaning they do—usually based on a made-up story). Nowhere in the Old Testament is such an adverb used to introduce etiological material. The writer wanted us to place the episode in the setting of the real world.

The link between verses 24-26 and the material before and after it is important. It is not that God is seeking Moses' life, as Pharaoh had. There are two key themes. First, there is the matter of the sons. Pharaoh's "firstborn" (v. 23) and Moses' son (perhaps his firstborn as well) are involved in a crucial contest that involves God's call to Israel, his "firstborn" (v. 22). The contrasts are deliberate, and they manifest the grace of God and a call for response to the word of God.

The second issue is the preparation of God's commissioned servant. God had prepared the nation of Israel, by virtue of their groaning, and he had prepared Moses in leadership skills; yet there was still the small but important matter of the preparation of the family. Moses had failed to have his son circumcised, either as a concession to his wife's scruples or because of his own relaxation of standards. As a result, he almost lost the opportunity to do what he had been prepared all his life to do—and he almost lost his life as well.

Obviously, Zipporah was moved to act quickly on her own. Without a word of instruction, she suddenly seized a flint knife (or stone) and circumcised her son. Usually this would be a ceremony performed by the head of the house. Zipporah's action shows that she instinctively connected her husband's malady with the failure to place their son under God's covenant through circumcision (Gen 17:10-14). Moses may well have been too ill to act on his own; therefore Zipporah took the initiative.

When Zipporah had excised the prepuce, she touched her husband's feet with it and said, with what must have been a tone of disgust and scorn, "Surely you are a bridegroom of blood to me." These words cannot be understood as communicating anything but derision and revulsion for the rite of circumcision.

There may well have been a long debate in this household over whether their son would be circumcised or not. Perhaps Zipporah argued that the operation struck her as repulsive. Moses may have countered, "But God commanded that we must circumcise all of our male children." In order to keep the peace, however, Moses may have let the matter drop and risked disobeying the command of God.

Just as he was preparing to return to Egypt and take up the mantle of leadership after a forty-year absence, however, Moses was suddenly struck down, faced with a peril that was clearly life-threatening. Zipporah knew immediately wherein the problem lay, so she acted with haste. Yet she was still unpersuaded about the rightness of the act. She complied under duress, not with a willing heart.

Moses plays no active part in this narrative at all. Some have attempted to argue that he had neglected his own circumcision, since he had spent all those years in Pharaoh's palace and then in Midian. But there is nothing in the text to confirm this idea. It is true, of course, that the Egyptians practiced a form of adult circumcision, but some contend that it was a partial circumcision only. In any case, Scripture does not make an issue of Moses' own circumcision.

If the scenario we have offered is reasonably close to what did indeed take place, then how can we defend God's intent to kill Moses? Even putting it mildly, this sounds most bizarre and extreme.

The syntax of Old Testament Hebrew tends to be unconcerned with secondary causes; thus, what God *permitted* is often said in the Old Testament to be done directly *by* him. Thus if, as we believe, God permitted Moses to be afflicted with a severe sickness, or some other danger, the proper way to express that in Hebrew language patterns would be to say that God wanted to kill him. It was not simply that Moses was sick and near death; it was a case of the sovereignty of God, who controls all events and happenings on planet earth. Thus the secondary causes were not important. The ultimate cause took precedence as a means of explanation.

Three Generations of Levites During 430 Years in Egypt

*These were the names of the sons of Levi according
to their records: Gershon, Kohath and Merari.
Levi lived 137 years. . . . The sons of Kohath were Amram,
Izhar, Hebron and Uzziel. Kohath lived 133 years. . . .
Amram married his father's sister Jochebed,
who bore him Aaron and Moses. Amram lived 137 years.*
EXODUS 6:16-20

*Now the length of time the Israelite people lived
in Egypt was 430 years.*
EXODUS 12:40

T*he genealogical lists in the Old Testament have been a source of* special delight and enormous difficulty. In a positive sense, they express a sense of order and attachment to history. These were real people who lived in real times with real family connections.

The difficulty is that all too many interpreters have been tempted to assume that these genealogies are complete lists of names and figures. Therefore, we can simply add up all the ages and obtain absolute dates for a number of prepatriarchal events for which we otherwise would have no data. Unfortunately, the assumption is faulty. These are not complete genealogical records, and it was not the writers' intention to provide this material for readers who might wish to add up numbers. Usually what the text is reluctant to do, we must be reluctant to do as well.

So we must ask, Is there evidence that these genealogies were condensed through the omission of less important names? In particular, can we determine whether there were only four generations from Levi to Moses during the 430 years of bondage in Egypt? Were Amram and Jochebed Aaron and Moses' immediate parents? If not, why does the text say Jochebed "bore him [Amram] Aaron and Moses?" (Ex 6:20). On the other hand, why does Exodus 2:1 remain noncommittal about the names of Moses' parents—"Now a man of the house of Levi married a Levite woman, and she became pregnant and gave birth to a son [Moses]"?

A parallel genealogy for the same period of time—from the days just before the twelve brothers went to Egypt until they came out 430 years later—is preserved in the line of Bezaleel, the artisan who worked on the tabernacle in 1 Chronicles 2:18-20. That record lists seven, not just four, lines of Moses, from Jacob to Bezaleel. This fact, that those 430 years embraced more than four generations, is confirmed by Joshua's genealogy in 1 Chronicles 7:23-27: there are *eleven* links between Jacob and Joshua, the latter being a younger contemporary of Moses.

The logical conclusion is that Moses' genealogy is condensed. It is inconceivable that there should be eleven links between Jacob and Joshua and only four or five between Jacob and Moses.

But if more proof is needed, we have it. An altogether overwhelming set of data can be seen in Numbers 3:19, 27-28. If no abridgment is understood in the four generations of Moses' ancestry, what results is this unbelievable set of numbers: the grandfather of Moses had, during Moses' lifetime, 8,600 male descendants (forget, for the moment, the females!), 2,750 of whom were between the ages of thirty and fifty (Num 4:36)! Now, all of us know that these were times of large families; but honestly, is it possible to make sense of what has been reported in these texts—unless there is considerable condensing and compression of the record to get at just the key characters?

Another piece of evidence is to be found in the fact that Levi's son Kohath was born before Jacob and his twelve sons went down to Egypt (Gen 46:11), where the emerging nation of Israel lived for 430 years (Ex 12:40). Now if Moses was 80 years old at the exodus (Ex 7:7), he must have been born 350 years after Kohath, who, as a consequence, could not have been his own grandfather. In fact, Kohath lived a total of 133 years, and his son Amram lived 137 years. These two numbers together, 270, do not add up to the 350 years needed to account for the 430 years in Egypt minus Moses' 80 years at the time of the exodus. What has happened, then, to Moses' genealogy? Unquestionably, Levi was Jacob's son. Likewise, Kohath was born to Levi before they went down to Egypt. There is also a strong possibility that Amram was the immediate descendant of Kohath. The missing links do not appear to come between Jacob and Levi, Levi and Kohath, or even Kohath and Amram.

But if the gaps come after Amram, why does Exodus 6:20 specifically say that Jochebed "bore" Moses to Amram? In the genealogies, such expressions are routinely used to say that individuals were descended from grandparents or even great-great-grandparents. A case in point is Genesis 46:18, where the sons of Zilpah, her grandsons and her great-grandsons are listed as "children *born* to Jacob *by Zilpah* . . . sixteen in all." Genesis 46:25 makes the same type of reckoning for the descendants of Bilhah. Therefore, the phrases "son of," "bore to," "born to" and "father of" have a wider range of meaning in Scripture than they have in contemporary Western usage. If we are to understand Scripture, we must accept the usage of the Hebrew writers of that time.

Some will point to Leviticus 10:4 and note that Uzziel, Amram's brother, is called "the uncle of Aaron." The Hebrew word translated "uncle," though applicable to a definite degree of relationship, has a wider scope of meaning, both etymologically and in its usage. A great-great-great-granduncle is still an uncle in biblical usage of the term.

It is fair to conclude, then, that this is why Exodus 2:1 does not supply us with the names of the Levitical couple who were the parents of Aaron and Moses. This example should alert us not to use genealogical lists in an attempt to obtain absolute dates for events and persons. Amram and Jochebed were not the immediate parents of Aaron and Moses. How many generations intervened we cannot tell. All that must be known for the purposes of revelation, however, has been disclosed.

There is selection and arrangement in the list that appears in Exodus 6:14-25. It includes only three of Jacob's twelve sons— Reuben, Simeon and Levi. It is framed by the near-verbatim repetition of verses 10-13 in verses 26-30, and the first part of verse 14 in the last part of verse 25. Clearly, its purposes are theological, not chronological or numerical.

No Idols in the Form of Anything

You shall not make for yourself an idol in the form
of anything in heaven above or on the earth beneath or in
the waters below. You shall not bow down to them or worship them;
for I, the LORD your God, am a jealous God, punishing
the children for the sin of the fathers to the third and fourth generation
of those who hate me, but showing love to a thousand
generations of those who love me and keep my commandments.
EXODUS 20:4-6

Was this second of the Ten Commandments intended to stifle any or all forms of artistic expression in Israel, and even in our own day? Is the depiction of any of God's creatures or any aspect of his creation strictly forbidden, whether it be by means of oil painting or sculpting in wood, stone, clay, silver or gold?

Does this text also teach that children may be expected to pay for the sins of their evil parents, regardless of their own lifestyle or personal ethics and practices? And are some children shown great love and kindness simply because one of their relatives loved God and kept his commandments?

Exodus 20:3, generally regarded as the first commandment, deals with internal worship of God. The third commandment, verse 7, deals with the spoken worship of God and the proper use of the tongue.

Verses 4-6 of Exodus 20 has to do with external worship of God. Covered in this second commandment are both the mode of worshiping God (vv. 4-5) and the penalty for failing to do so (vv. 5-6). The prohibition is clearly aimed at the sin of idolatry.

The Old Testament is replete with synonyms and words for idols; in fact, it has fourteen such words. The word *idol* used here refers to an actual statue, while the word *form* or *resemblance* applies to real or imagined pictorial representations of any sort.

But neither term is used in this context to speak to the question of what is or is not legitimate artistic expression. The context addresses the matter of worship—and only that. It is wrong to use the second commandment to forbid or curtail the visual or plastic arts.

The commandment speaks instead to the issue of using images that would, in effect, rival God. The actual proscription is, "You shall not bow down to them or worship them." Here two expressions ("bow down" and "worship"), in a figure of speech called *hendiadys*, are used to convey a single idea: do not use images to offer religious worship to the living God. The worshiper must not compromise that worship by having a concrete center for that worship. Such a practice would be too close to what the heathen were doing.

This prohibition must be viewed against the background of Egyptian religion, for Israel had just emerged from its bondage in Egypt. Egyptian worship was directed toward the heavenly bodies, especially the sun, and such creatures as birds, cows, frogs and fish. Thus what is forbidden is not the making of images of fish, birds, bulls or the like. Instead, it is forbidden to make an *image of God* with a view to using it as part of one's worship. Such substitutes would only steal hearts and minds away from the true worship of God.

Should further support be needed for this restriction of work in the plastic or visual forms only when such art pieces would be used to stand in for God, one need only remember what the Lord commanded with regard to the tabernacle. Under divine direction, all sorts of representations of the created order were included in this structure and its accouterments. Had all such representations been wrong, Scripture would have contradicted itself.

The penalty or sanction that follows the second commandment's proscription begins with the magisterial reminder that "I, the LORD your God, am a jealous God." God's "jealousy" does not involve being suspicious or wrongfully envious of the success of others, or even mistrusting. When used of God, the word *jealous* refers to that quality of his character that demands exclusive devotion to all that is just, right and fair. Jealousy is the anger that God directs against all that opposes him. It is also the energy he expends in vindicating those who believe in the rightness of this quality and of his name.

God's jealousy, or his zeal, is that emotion by which he is stirred up against whatever hinders the enjoyment of what he loves and desires. Therefore, the greatest insult against God's love for us is to slight that love and to choose instead a lesser or baser love. That is idolatry. It is a spiritual form of adultery that results in neglect, substitution and finally contempt for the public and private worship of God.

When children repeat the crimes and sins of their parents, they clearly show that they hate God. But this does not mean they are predetermined to follow a path they actually wish to avoid. Deuteronomy 24:16 makes it clear that "fathers shall not be put to death for their children, nor children put to death for their fathers; each is to die for his own sin." No child would ever suffer *eternal* condemnation because of what his or her parents had done (or vice versa). *Temporal* punishments may come to children because of their parents' or their nation's guilt, or because another's name was filched by fraud and extortion (see, for example, 1 Kings 21:21-22, 29).

But it was only when children agreed with their parents' sin—seconding, as it were, their parents' original motion—and "hated" God that the effects continued to be felt for several generations. Apparently, each succeeding generation fell into the trap of hating God that had been set by their ancestors.

Yet consider how long-lasting are the effects of love for God and his commandments. These blessings last for numerous generations—"thousands," according to verse 6. So the effects of disobedience last for some time, but not nearly as long as the effects of obedience.

No, this commandment does not prohibit artistic representations of the created world. It does, however, prohibit the use of images that call our hearts and minds away from focusing on the one true and living God, who is spirit and not like any of the shapes and forms that he created.

· CHAPTER 16 ·

Remember the Sabbath Day to Keep It Holy

Remember the Sabbath day by keeping it holy.
Six days you shall labor and do all your work,
but the seventh day is a Sabbath to the LORD your God.
On it you shall not do any work, neither you, nor your son
or daughter, nor your manservant or maidservant,
nor your animals, nor the alien within your gates.
For in six days the LORD made the heavens and the earth,
the sea, and all that is in them, but he rested on the seventh day.
Therefore the LORD blessed the Sabbath day and made it holy.
EXODUS 20:8-11

T*here are a number of questions connected with the fourth command-*ment. It is not the meaning of the words of this commandment that makes it a hard saying, but the application of its meaning to today.

Do the origins of a sabbath day lie in the Babylonian concept of such a sabbath on the seventh, fourteenth, twenty-first and twenty-eighth day? Does the name "sabbath" come from the

Babylonian *shabatu*, the fifteenth day of the Babylonian month? Were these days of rest in Babylon, or did they have some other meaning?

In our day, how seriously must we take the command to reserve one day each week, and on that day to avoid all forms of work done on the other six days? Is this command purely ceremonial in its origins, or does it have moral force? Further, does this command represent the law of Moses from which the Christian is freed, since it reflects forms and ceremonies that were done away with when Christ died on the cross? And what relation, if any, does the seventh-day injunction have to do with the new first day of worship set up by several New Testament texts?

Since this command begins with the word *remember*, it is clear that the sabbath day already existed prior to this Mosaic legislation. Exodus 20:11 connects it with the work pattern of the Creator, who took six "days" to create the world and then rested on the seventh day. His example is meant to be normative and therefore transcends all local custom, cultures and ceremonies of Mosaic legislation.

As for the claim that the whole concept comes from the Babylonians, it needs to be pointed out that they did not call their seventh, fourteenth, twenty-first and twenty-eighth days "days of rest." Actually, these were "evil" or "unlucky" days when it was best not to do anything so as to avoid harm. Superstitious fear can hardly be equated with a theology of rest.

Likewise, the name "sabbath" did not originate with the Babylonians, for its Hebrew etymology is related to the semantic field of *shabat*, meaning "to rest" or "to cease." In the Old Testament, the sabbath was a day of cessation, for religious reasons, from the normal routine of life. In the Babylonian culture, there was a mid-month day—unrelated to the pattern of seven—called *shabatu*, meaning "the day of the stilling of the heart," that is, the heart of the gods. The Babylonians themselves made no connection between the pattern of the seventh, fourteenth, twenty-first and twenty-eighth days and this fifteenth day.

Now if this ordinance goes back to creation and has as its purpose imitation of the Lord himself, what shall we say of its continuing relevance for us? Was there any indication, even in the Old Testament itself, that the day set apart to the Lord might be changed from the seventh to the first, as many Christians say today?

To take the latter question first, yes, there is such evidence. In Leviticus 23:15, during the Feast of Weeks, the day after the sabbath had significance along with the sabbath itself. Israel was to count off fifty days, up to the day of the seventh sabbath; then, on "the day after the seventh Sabbath," they were to present an offering of new grain to the Lord (Lev 23:15-16). Again on this "eighth day" Israel was to hold another "sacred assembly and present an offering made to the LORD by fire" (Lev 23:36). "The first day is a sacred assembly; do no regular work," the Lord said (Lev 23:35), and on the eighth day, when the closing assembly was held, they were again to do no work. "The first day is a day of rest, and the eighth day also is a day of rest" (Lev 23:39). Since the Feast of Booths or Tabernacles cannot be properly celebrated until the time of Israel's kingdom rest—after they have once again been regathered in their land from all over the world—it is clear that this passage looks forward to the eternal state and the rest of all, when the tabernacle of God is once again with humanity (Rev 21:3).

These arguments, along with the fact that the early church worshiped on the first day of the week, fit the prediction of an eighth-day (that is, first-day-of-the-week) Sabbath very well (1 Cor 16:2; Rev 1:10; Acts 20:7). Justin Martyr (c. A.D. 150) indicates in his *Apology* 1.67-68 that in his day offerings were being brought to the church on Sunday—the first day of the week.

Many will still argue, "Isn't this law a ceremonial piece of legislation from which we as believers are exempt?"

Actually, the fourth commandment is both ceremonial and moral. It is ceremonial in that it specifies the seventh day. It is moral because there is a sanctity of time; it sets aside a portion of time for the worship and service of God as well as for the refreshment and recuperation of human beings.

God is the Lord of time. As such, he has a legitimate right to claim a proportion of our time, just as he has a claim on a proportion of our money and our talents.

The fourth commandment's prohibition of any forms of normal work on the seventh day was so seriously regarded that it affected not only all members of the Israelite household but also all aliens residing in the land and even the country's cattle.

The book of Hebrews, of course, continues to argue on the basis of the relevance of the sabbath rest for the people of God. This sabbath still remains. It is a "stop" day, picturing the millennial rest of God that is to come when Christ returns the second time to rule and reign with his saints.

This commandment must not be lightly regarded as a piece of antique history or as conventional wisdom that may be used as one sees fit. Rather, it calls for an imitation of God's own action, and it carries a blessing for all who will observe it.

You
Shall Not
Kill

You shall not murder.
EXODUS 20:13

Is the sixth commandment a prohibition against the taking of all forms of life in any manner whatsoever? Or is it limited to the taking of human life, as the NIV translation suggests? And if it is limited to the taking of human life, is that prohibition under all circumstances, by all methods, for all causes and in all times?

The Hebrew language possesses seven words related to killing, and the word used in this sixth commandment appears only forty-seven times in the Old Testament. This Hebrew verb, *ratsach*, refers only to the killing of a person, never to killing animals and not even to killing persons in a war. It carries no implications of the means of killing.

If any one of the seven words for killing in the Old Testament signifies what we refer to as "murder," this is the verb. It implies premeditation and intentionality. Without exception, especially in the later Old Testament periods, it refers to intentional, violent murder (Ps 94:6; Prov 22:13; Is 1:21; Hos 4:2; 6:9; Jer 7:9). In each instance, the act was conceived in the mind first and the victim was chosen deliberately.

Thus the Old Testament would never use this verb to denote the killing of beasts for food (Gen 9:6) or the nation's involvement in a war commanded by God. It would, however, use this verb in reference to self-murder (suicide), in reference to the actions of accessories to a murder (2 Sam 12:9) and in reference to those who have authority to punish known murderers, but who fail to use this authority though guilt has been proved beyond any reasonable doubt (2 Kings 21:19).

Some have pointed out that some uses of this verb relate simply to blood vengeance and the role of the avenger. Vengeance, they would argue, is different from murder, with its premeditation and intentionality.

In the Old Testament, however, both murder and blood vengeance incur blood guilt, which is viewed as polluting the land and requiring atonement (Num 35:16, 25; Deut 4:41-43; Josh 20:3). The only atonement available is either execution of the murderer or, in the case of the avenger of blood, the death (by natural causes) of the high priest (Num 35:27-28, 30-31).

Note that Numbers 35:31 specifically distinguishes the capital offense of murder from the almost twenty other offenses punishable by death. Jewish and modern interpreters have long held that since this verse prohibited taking a "ransom for the life of a murderer"—a substitute of some kind—in all the other cases, a substitution could be made for the death penalty. But so serious was murder that the death penalty was to be enforced.

In cases of nighttime invasion of a household by burglars, the prohibition in this verse did not apply, and *ratsach* is not the verb used (Ex 22:2). Nor does this commandment apply to accidental killings—that is, cases of manslaughter (Deut 19:5)—or to the execution of murderers by the recognized arm of the state (Gen 9:6).

Life was so sacred to God that all violent forms of taking human life caused guilt to fall upon the land. This was true of both manslaughter and premeditated murder. Both forms of killing demanded some type of atonement, as mentioned already.

The reason life was so valuable was that men and women are made in the image of God. To kill a person was to kill God in effigy. That is why the life of the murderer was owed to God, not to the bereaved relatives of the victim or to society. Capital punishment for first-degree murder was, and continues to be, mandated because God honors his image in all humanity. To fail to carry out this mandate is ultimately to attack the value, worth and dignity of all. It undermines other struggles as well, including those for racial equality, women's rights, civil rights and human embryo rights—all are equally based on the fact that persons are made in the "image of God."

The covenant code of Exodus 21:12, 28-32 shows how this sixth commandment was put into practice. A person or animal that caused the death of another person was to be put to death. In another law in this code, even the fetus is regarded as human and viable; when it was killed, the life of the murderer was required (Ex 21:22-25).

Life was and remains sacred to the Giver of life. Under no circumstances was one to take one's own life or lie in wait to take someone else's life. So valuable was life, however fallen, that the only way to cleanse the evil caused by killing was atonement before God. Each murder placed blood-guilt on the land until it was solved and atoned for.

· C H A P T E R 1 8 ·

Moses, Aaron and the Seventy Elders Saw God

*Moses and Aaron, Nadab and Abihu, and the seventy elders of Israel
went up and saw the God of Israel. Under his feet was something
like a pavement made of sapphire, clear as the sky itself.
But God did not raise his hand against these leaders of the Israelites;
they saw God, and they ate and drank.*
EXODUS 24:9-11

*Then Moses said, "Now show me your glory." And the Lord said,
"I will cause all my goodness to pass in front of you,
and I will proclaim my name, the LORD, in your presence. . . .
But," he said, "you cannot see my face, for no one may see me and live."*
EXODUS 33:18-20

T he claim that Moses and his company "saw the God of Israel"
appears to contradict the flat denials of such a possibility in texts
such as Exodus 33:20. John 1:18 affirms that "no one has ever
seen God, but God the One and Only [the only Son], who is at
the Father's side, has made him known." Similarly, 1 Timothy
6:16 teaches that God is the one "who alone is immortal and who
lives in unapproachable light, whom no one has seen or can see."

What are we to believe then? Did some see God who is spirit and without form, or did they not? These passages surely look as if they contradict each other.

Exodus 24:9-11 constitutes some of the most astonishing and almost inexplicable verses in the Old Testament. The translators who compiled the Greek version of the Old Testament, the Septuagint, were so concerned about any wrong connotations in this verse that they added "in the place where he stood" to the words "they saw the God of Israel." There is no basis for such an addition, however, except the tendency of this translation to avoid any descriptions of God in terms that are used of human beings (the so-called antianthropomorphic trend of the LXX).

Even though verse 10 clearly says that the leaders "saw the God of Israel," the text does not go on to describe him any more than did Isaiah when he saw Adonai exalted in the (heavenly) temple (Is 6). The verb used in verse 10 is used of seeing with one's eyes. Only when we get to verse 11 is there a qualification, for it uses another verb that means "to see in a vision."

Moreover, despite the assertion that Moses and the leaders saw God, the description of what they saw is of what was at his feet, not the appearance of God himself. It could well be that the group were not given permission to lift their faces toward God, but saw only the pavement beneath his feet. Maybe that is what the Greek translators were attempting to get at when they added the phrase we've mentioned.

When Moses asked to be shown the glory of God, he was refused on the grounds that humans cannot see the face of God and live (Ex 33:18-20). In the earlier text, since no request to see God's glory is cited, we must assume that what Moses and his companions experienced was a theophany of the presence of God.

Even what little they saw of the setting of God's presence so humbled and awed them that they apparently flung themselves down in an act of obeisance. Hence, what they saw and reported was no higher than the level of the pavement. In spite of the uniqueness and unnaturalness of this experience, Moses and his companions were not harmed or disciplined by God; he "did not raise his hand" against them (v. 11). But they did experience a special nearness to God as they partook together of a covenantal meal.

We conclude that no one *has* ever seen God except the Son. What Moses, Aaron, Nadab, Abihu and the seventy elders experienced was the real presence of God and the place where he stood. When God is said to have shown his "back" or his "face" to any in those days or later, it is an anthropomorphic usage— a description of God in terms used of humans so as to point to a definite reality, but only in ways that approximate that reality. God's "back" suggests his disapproval, and his "face" suggests his blessing and smile of approval. But in no sense can these terms be used to denote any shape or form of God.

Repeatedly, even in the Old Testament, believers were told that no one may see God and live (Judg 6:22-23; 13:22; Is 6:5). Even when Moses is said to have seen the "back" of God in Exodus 33:23, the translation should rather be that what he saw was the "afterburn" or the "effects" that the passing of God's glory left on the scene. God certainly does not have a "back" or posterior parts, as some imagine from this odd translation found almost universally in English translations. Note that Moses was told to hide himself in the cleft of the rock. Then, as God protected him with his covering hand, God caused all the divine glory to pass before him. What Moses was allowed to see was the afterglow that the glory had left, for even a direct view of God's glory would have been too much for Moses.

So God remains unseen, but mightily able to manifest the reality and majesty of his presence.

• C H A P T E R 1 9 •

The Camel, the Coney and the Rabbit Chew the Cud

You may eat any animal that has a split hoof completely divided and that chews the cud. There are some that only chew the cud or only have a split hoof, but you must not eat them. The camel, though it chews the cud, does not have a split hoof; it is ceremonially unclean for you. The coney, though it chews the cud, does not have a split hoof; it is unclean for you. The rabbit, though it chews the cud, does not have a split hoof; it is unclean for you.
LEVITICUS 11:3-6

Do the animals listed in Leviticus 11:3-6 actually "chew the cud" in the scientific sense of having a gastronomical system wherein several stomachs are used for processing food?

True ruminants generally have four stomachs. As the stomachs work, the food is regurgitated into the mouth, where it is chewed up again. Do the camel, coney and rabbit qualify as ruminants? If not, how do we explain the presence of this classification here?

Cows, sheep and goats "chew the cud." They swallow their food, without chewing it especially fine, and store it in one of their stomach compartments. Later, at leisure, they bring it up and rechew it more thoroughly, again swallowing it. Clearly, the Hebrews were not working with this definition of "chewing the cud." The camel, coney and rabbit are also said to "chew the cud," but these animals only appear to chew their food as the true ruminants do. In the technical sense neither the hyrax (Hebrew *sapan*, or *Hyrax syriacus)* of Leviticus 11:5—which is also called the "coney" in the King James Version and New International Version and the "rock badger" in the New American Standard Bible—nor the rabbit in Leviticus 11:6 "chews the cud."

The Hebrew expression for "chew the cud" is literally "raising up what has been swallowed." But what does this raising up of what has been swallowed refer to? Surely there is the appearance of a cud-chewing process in these animals. In fact, so convincing was this appearance that Carolus Linnaeus (1707-1778), to whom we owe the modern system of biological classification, at first classified the coney and the hare as ruminants.

We believe the rule in Leviticus should be understood not according to later scientific refinements of classification; instead, it was based on simple observation. The fact that the camel, the coney and the rabbit go through motions similar to those of cows, sheep and goats must take precedence over the fact that we later limited the "cud-chewing" category to just animals that have four stomachs. The modern definition of terms does not take away from Moses' ability, or even his right, to use words as he sees fit to use them. To question his use of a term to which Linnaeus eventually gave a more restrictive meaning is anachronistic argumentation.

Interestingly, resting hares and rabbits do go through a process that is very similar to what we moderns call "chewing the cud." The process is called "refection." As the hare rests, it passes droppings of different composition, which it once again eats. Thus the hare is chewing without taking fresh greens into its mouth. During this second passage of the food through its stomach, that which had been indigestible can be better assimilated through the action of bacteria.

The case of the three animals that "chewed the cud" in Moses' day but no longer do so can be solved. Moses' classification had a solid observational basis that was accessible to all. In modern times, the phrase "chewing the cud" has been given a more restrictive meaning. Later generations, having forgotten which came first, have tended to freeze the meaning to the most recent definition and then to accuse Moses of not using the term in this later sense. Case solved.

· C H A P T E R 2 0 ·

The Goat Shall Be Sent into the Desert as a Scapegoat

Then [Aaron] is to take the two goats and present
them before the LORD at the entrance to the Tent of Meeting.
He is to cast lots for the two goats—one lot for the LORD
and the other for the scapegoat. Aaron shall bring the goat whose
lot falls to the LORD and sacrifice it for a sin offering.
But the goat chosen by lot as the scapegoat shall be presented
alive before the LORD to be used for making atonement
by sending it into the desert as a scapegoat.
LEVITICUS 16:7-10

What is the "scapegoat" of the Day of Atonement in Leviticus 16? Why do some scholars say that this goat was offered to Azazel, a desert demon that was capable of feeding on an animal laden with the sins of the entire nation of Israel? Does the Old Testament actually give aid and comfort to such crass views and teach that demons inhabit the desert?

And if the demon view is true, why does Leviticus 17:7 expressly forbid making offerings or sacrifices to demons? Also, what is the meaning of the Hebrew name used in connection with the scapegoat, *azazel?* Is this name to be connected with other demons named in Scripture such as Lilith, "the night hag" (Is 34:14), or the Shedim, "demons" (Lev 17:7; 2 Chron 11:15; Is 13:21; 34:14), literally "the hairy ones," "satyrs" or "goat idols"?

No day was, or continues to be, as sacred to the Jewish community as Yom Kippur, the Day of Atonement. After Aaron, the high priest, had made atonement for his own sins and those of his household, he proceeded with the rites of atonement for the whole community. The community brought two male goats as one sin offering and a ram as a burnt offering. Both goats were for atonement: one dealt with the fact of atonement and the other with the effect of atonement in removing sin. The first goat had to be slain in order to picture the atonement proferred; the other goat was presented alive and then released into the wilderness, symbolizing the removal of the forgiven sins (on the basis of the slain substitute).

Thus far all interpreters tend to agree, but after this point disagreement breaks out. First of all, it has been pointed out that the name for the goats is not the standard term, but the expression that is used always in connection with the sin offering *(she'ir 'izzim*—Lev 4:23-24, 28; 5:6; 9:3; 23:19).

But the most difficult specification to deal with is that as the two goats are placed at the entrance to the Tent of Meeting— the tabernacle—and the lots are drawn, one goat is said to be "for the LORD," and the other lot falls "for azazel" (Lev 16:8—*leYahweh; la'aza'zel).*

The Greek translators did not regard *azazel* as a proper name, but connected it with *'azal,* a verb that does not appear in the Old Testament. The meaning they gave it was "to send away." Hence the full meaning of the Hebrew expression would be "in order to send away." The Latin translation followed this same understanding. But, it is objected, this meaning will not easily fit the contexts of the last part of verse 10 and the first part of verse 26.

In later Jewish theology, the apocryphal book of Enoch uses Azazel as the name for one of the fallen angels. But there is no evidence for the existence of a demon by that name in Moses' day. Enoch's elaborate demonology is admittedly late (c. 200 B.C.) and often uses the late Aramaic forms for these names. It is clear that they are all of postbiblical invention.

The most adequate explanation is to view the term *azazel* as being composed of two words: the first part, *'az,* meaning "goat," and the second part *'azel,* meaning "to go away." With recent evidence from the Ugaritic (the language of ancient Canaan from which Hebrew is derived), compound names such as this one are turning up more frequently than what we had expected based on our Hebrew evidence. This is how the rendering "scapegoat" came to be. Today, however, we would need to call it the "escape-goat," for by "scapegoat" we mean the one who always gets blamed or gets stuck with a task that is distasteful. Originally, however, the King James translators meant "the goat that was led away."

Since this ceremony is part of one sin offering, in no sense is the second goat an offering to the devil or his demons. The arguments that are brought in to support the view that the second goat is for the devil or his demons are unconvincing. One says that since the first clause of verse 8 indicates that the goat is designated for a person—the Lord—the second clause also must refer to the goat's being designated for a person—Azazel. While this is a grammatical possibility, it is not required by the text. The specific prohibition of making such offerings to demons, found in Leviticus 17:7, is decisive, however, in ruling out this possibility.

According to another argument, the words in 16:10 cannot mean that atonement is being made *with* azazel (that is, azazel as the scapegoat) to propitiate the Lord, but rather that atonement is being made to propitiate Azazel (that is, Azazel as a wilderness demon). The reply is that the same Hebrew expression for atonement is used throughout the chapter. Moreover, in Exodus 30:10 the same expression is translated "to atone over, or upon." Here, the high priest was to make atonement "over" the scapegoat, by putting Israel's guilt upon it and then sending it away. If the expression appears strange, the answer is that the act described is itself unusual, and no other word could fit it better.

The high priest did not atone for sin by making an offering to Satan or to his demons. There is evidence that the Old Testament teaches the existence of demons, for Deuteronomy 32:17 and Psalm 106:37 speak of such beings. But in no sense were the Israelites ever told to sacrifice to them; as we have seen, Leviticus 17:7 specifically warns against such sacrifices.

Moses Was More Humble Than Anyone Else

Now Moses was a very humble man,
more humble than anyone else
on the face of the earth.
NUMBERS 12:3

Numbers 12:3 is the most difficult text in the whole book of Numbers. Critical scholars (and others) have correctly observed that it is rather unlikely that a truly humble person would write in such a manner about himself, even if he actually felt the statement was true. Many critical scholars are so convinced of the inappropriateness of recording such a note about oneself that they have used this as a strong mark against the Mosaic authorship of the whole book.

One scholar has suggested recently that the word translated "humble" or "meek" should be translated instead "miserable." The idea of "miserable" certainly would fit the context of this chapter very well. To be sure, Moses had a most unmanageable task. He had just said in Numbers 11:14, "It is too much!" With all the attacks on his family, he may have passed into a deep depression. Thus, a very good translation possibility is, "Now Moses was exceedingly miserable, more than anyone on the face of the earth!"

Those who retain the meaning "humble" usually cite this passage, along with other passages such as the Deuteronomy 34 announcement of Moses' death and burial site, as evidences for post-Mosaic additions authorized by the Spirit of God to the inspired text. Normally, Joshua is credited with contributing these comments under the direction of the Spirit of God. Joshua 24:26 says, "And Joshua recorded these things in the Book of the Law of God"—a clear reference to the five books of the Law, whose authorship is usually ascribed to Moses.

This is the view that I favor, though the first idea of translating the word as "miserable" is a good second solution and one that passes all the tests we can give it.

Moses, of course, was not a naturally "meek" man. If he became so, he learned it through the trials he had to experience as the leader of a very stubborn group of people.

Some have argued for Moses' authorship of the verse, reminding us that the apostle Paul was compelled by challenges to his apostleship to point his own excellence of character in 2 Corinthians 11:5 and 12:11-12. But it does not seem that Moses was facing exactly the same set of circumstances.

Biblical writers speak of themselves with an objectivity that is rarely matched in other pieces of literature. Their self-references usually lay bare their sins and failures. It is rare for them to praise themselves.

The translators of the New International Version were no doubt justified placing this verse in parentheses. The note is a later parenthetical remark made under the direction of the Holy

Spirit by Joshua, at the time he was writing his own book. Rather than a brief slippage in revelation in which one of God's servants suddenly indulged in a bit of braggadocio, it is a note that God directed his servant Joshua to add to the Book of the Law.

Phinehas Drove a Spear Through Both of Them

> When Phinehas son of Eleazar, the son of Aaron, the priest,
> saw [the Israelite Zimri bringing the Midianite woman Cozbi into
> his tent], he left the assembly, took a spear in his hand and followed
> the Israelite into the tent. He drove the spear through both of them. . . .
> Then the plague against the Israelites was stopped. . . . The Lord said
> to Moses, "Phinehas . . . has turned my anger away from the Israelites;
> for he was as zealous as I am for my honor among them, so that
> in my zeal I did not put an end to them. . . . He was zealous for
> the honor of his God and made atonement for the Israelites."
>
> NUMBERS 25:7-13

Several questions are generally raised in connection with this most unusual story of Phinehas. The first involves the action of Cozbi
and Zimri. What were they doing that so stirred the holy indig-
nation of Phinehas that he impaled both of them with one thrust
of his spear?

We will need to understand what was involved in the worship
of Baal of Peor (Num 25:1-5). And was Israel's lapse into this sin

in any way connected with the advice or at the instigation of Balaam, the son of Beor?

Finally, we wish to know how the death of the couple, Zimri and Cozbi, could effect an atonement and assuage the wrath of God. All of these questions arise from one of the most bizarre episodes in Israel's long wilderness wanderings.

At this point, Israel was encamped at Shittim, or Acacia. It was a site east of the Jordan and six miles north of the Dead Sea, if this name is to be connected with modern Tel el-Kefrein.

It appears that the Israelite men began to have sexual relations with the Moabite and Midianite women (Num 25:1, 6). How such liaisons began we can only guess, but they seem to be connected with the bad advice given to the Moabites by the prophet Balaam, son of Beor. Prior to this event, the king of Moab had hired Balaam to curse the people of Israel; because of the strong hand of God on his life, however, Balaam had only been able to bless them. Apparently still bent on helping the Moabite king, Balaam had stayed on in the land of Moab and Midian. Numbers 31:16 informs us that "[the Midianite women] were the ones who followed Balaam's advice and were the means of turning the Israelites away from the LORD in what happened at Peor, so that a plague struck the LORD's people." (Apparently, the Midianites were in Moab giving military advice to the Moabites at this time.)

The Moabites worshiped the war god Chemosh, but they must have also indulged in the fertility religion of Baal. This cult was marked by some of the most depraved religious practices in Canaan. In lurid and orgiastic rites, the worshipers would emulate the sacred prostitution of their gods and goddesses, often also participating in a ceremonial meal. In the case of Baal of Peor, we suspect that the cult also involved veneration for the dead. "Peor" may be the Hebrew and Phoenician spelling for the Luwian *Pahura*. This word in Hittite means "fire" and may derive from some form of the root that underlies the Greek *pyr*, "fire."

Among the Israelites, then, the Midianite and Moabite women continued to prostrate themselves in Baal worship, imitating fertility rituals. And one day, as all the Israelites were gathered in front of the tabernacle confessing their sin, the son of one of the leaders in the tribe of Simeon paraded before them with a Moabite woman, headed for his tent.

Reading the situation clearly, Phinehas swung into action. By the time he reached them in the back (bedroom) part of the tent, the couple were already involved in sexual intercourse. With a single thrust, Phinehas speared both of them. His action stopped the plague that had broken out among the Israelites.

Israel's wholesale embracing of the immorality and idolatry of pagan ritualistic sex had aroused the anger of God. While God had saved Israel from the curses of Balaam, the Israelites could not save themselves from sinning against God.

Phinehas was no vigilante. He was heir apparent to the priesthood; thus he, no doubt, was one of the appointed judges whom Moses had ordered to slay all known offenders. This story does not justify the actions of private persons who, under the guise of zeal for expediting God's purposes, take matters into their own hands when they see wrongdoing rather than contacting the appropriate authorities.

Because of the Israelites' apostasy and sin, atonement was required before divine forgiveness could be proffered. The atonement that Phinehas offered was that of two human offenders.

Normally in the Old Testament, atonement is mentioned in connection with sacrifices, such as the sin offering. But in twenty-two passages, atonement was effected by means other than ceremonial offerings (for example, Ex 32:30-32; Deut 21:1-9; 2 Sam 21:3-9). Therefore, just as the life of the animal was a substitute, the means of ransoming the life of the guilty party, so the holiness of God was defended in this case through the substitution of the lives of the sinning couple. With atonement made, God could pardon his people and halt the spread of the plague.

The reward given to Phinehas was that his descendants would enjoy eternal possession of the priesthood. That priesthood continued, except for the interval of the priesthood of Eli, without interruption until the collapse of the nation in 586 B.C.

Do Not Accept a Ransom for the Life of a Murderer

Do not accept a ransom for the life of a murderer,
who deserves to die. He must surely be put to death.
NUMBERS 35:31

Did the Old Testament allow vendetta and retaliation in its famous "eye for an eye and tooth for a tooth"? Did this same concept carry over into blood vengeance and all capital offenses?

Of the crimes punishable by death under Old Testament law, was it possible, as some claim, to obtain compensation for damages through some type of substitutionary restitution in every case except first-degree, premeditated murder? If so, why was this crime singled out for special treatment? Were not the other crimes as serious? If they were not, why did they carry such a stiff sanction—the death penalty?

The key text in this discussion must be Numbers 35:31, "Do not accept a ransom [= substitute] for the life of a murderer, who deserves to die. He must surely be put to death."

There are sixteen crimes that called for the death penalty in the Old Testament: kidnaping, adultery, homosexuality, incest, bestiality, incorrigible delinquency in a child, striking or cursing parents, offering a human sacrifice, false prophecy, blasphemy, profaning the sabbath, sacrificing to false gods, magic and divination, unchastity, the rape of a betrothed virgin and premeditated murder. In each case, where the evidence was clear and beyond a reasonable doubt, the death penalty was demanded.

One major distinction was drawn, however, between the penalty for premeditated murder and penalties for the other fifteen crimes on this list. Only in the case where someone had lain in wait to kill with malice and forethought does Scripture specify that the officials were forbidden to take a ransom.

The word *ransom* comes from a root meaning "substitute." The only fair inference from Number 35:31, then, is that perpetrators of any of the other fifteen capital crimes could escape death by offering a proper ransom or substitute. In those fifteen cases, the death penalty served to mark the seriousness of the crime. It is important, however, to note that only God could say which crimes might have their sanctions lessened.

Some have contended that this argument is an argument from silence, and therefore fallacious. But the alternative to this "argument from silence" (which has venerable precedent in rabbinic and Protestant commentary) would require upholding the death penalty for all sixteen crimes as valid to our present day. And if death is the only proper punishment for these crimes even in the present day, why did the apostle Paul not make any reference to it, especially when he had specific occasion to do so when he dealt with the case of incest in 1 Corinthians 5? Why did Paul recommend church discipline rather than capital punishment for the offending mother and son?

I am not arguing here that the penalties of the Old Testament are too severe or that the New Testament is more "urbane" and "cultured." Some have properly noted that even Hebrews 2:2 says that "every violation and disobedience received its just [or appropriate] punishment." In fact, too many people misunderstand the *talion* ("tooth-for-a-tooth") principle (Ex 21:23-25). It is simply a "life-for-life" stereotype expression that worked out in actual practice to this: Make the punishment fit the crime; don't try to profit from or to trade on calamity. The tooth-for-a-tooth and eye-for-an-eye would be contextualized today as bumper-for-bumper and fender-for-fender; but don't try to get next year's tuition or the price of a new Mercedes out of the accident as well!

Since the taking of life involved deep disregard for God and for the creatures made in his image, Genesis 9:6 makes it clear that the only way the state and society could preserve the rights, dignity and worth of all humanity was to offer the life of the proven first-degree murderer back to God. That is why this one capital offense remained when the others were allowed the option of a "ransom" or "substitute."

Write Her a Certificate of Divorce

*If a man marries a woman who becomes displeasing to him because
he finds something indecent about her, and he writes her a certificate
of divorce, gives it to her and sends her from his house, and if
after she leaves his house she becomes the wife of another man, and her
second husband dislikes her and writes her a certificate of divorce,
gives it to her and sends her from his house, or if he dies, then her first
husband, who divorced her, is not allowed to marry her again after she
has been defiled. That would be detestable in the eyes of the LORD. Do not bring
sin upon the land the LORD your God is giving you as an inheritance.*
DEUTERONOMY 24:1-4

Does *Deuteronomy 24:1-4 assert that a man must give a certificate*
of divorce to his wife if she displeases him? If not, why do the
Authorized Version (the King James), the American Standard
Version of 1901 and the English Revised Version say "he *shall*
write a bill of divorcement"?

Was divorce an intrinsic "right" or prerogative that had divine
approval and legitimation in Old Testament times? What becomes then of the teachings of Jesus in Mark 10:2-12 and the

apostle Paul in 1 Corinthians 7:10-16? All these questions continue to make Deuteronomy 24:1-4 a hard saying that demands some solid answers.

We must begin our answer by stating that Deuteronomy 24:1-4 does not bestow any divine approval, or even an implied approval, on divorce as such. It sought, rather, to soften some of the hardships and injustices that divorce caused for women in a society that persisted in this practice.

Unfortunately, the translators of the three above-mentioned English versions of this text failed to notice that verses 1-3 constitute a protasis (or conditional clause) whose apodosis (or resolution) comes only in verse 4. The significance of this syntax is that Moses did not make divorce mandatory. This passage does not authorize husbands to divorce their wives.

Rightly understood, the rule simply prohibits a husband from returning to a wife whom he had divorced after she has married a second time—even if her second husband has died in the interim.

The most difficult part of this Deuteronomy passage is the phrase "something indecent." Literally, it means "nakedness of a thing."

The offensive act of the wife against her husband, which he is using as his grounds for a divorce, can hardly be adultery. The Mosaic Law prescribed death for adultery (Lev 20:10; Deut 22:22). And when adultery was only suspected, but not proved, there were specified ways to handle such situations (Num 5:11-31). And this phrase cannot refer to a case where the wife was charged with previous sexual promiscuity, for that too had been anticipated (Deut 22:13-21). In none of these other cases does our phrase "something indecent" appear, nor is divorce set forth as the appropriate punishment for any of them.

The rabbis held vastly different opinions on the meaning of "something indecent." Rabbi Hillel taught that it referred to something repulsive—a physical defect, or even ruining a meal!

Rabbi Akiba interpreted it even more liberally: divorce could be "for any and every reason" (Mt 19:3), such as a man's finding another woman more attractive than his own wife. Others have believed that the phrase refers to some type of illness, for example, a skin disease.

Whatever the indecency was, it is clear that the common law allowed considerable latitude. The conclusion we are left with is that "something indecent" refers to some kind of improper behavior, short of illicit sexual intercourse.

But the precise definition actually matters little, since the Law is not prescribing divorce as a punishment here, only assuming that some divorces were being carried out on the basis of common law. The reason for divorce is not the point that this legislation aims to address. Deuteronomy 24:4 is more concerned about protecting the woman from exposure to the whims of a fickle or vindictive husband, who, without putting his declaration of divorce in writing, could resume or drop his married state—depending on what his sexual needs, laundry pile or desires for a good meal were!

What is taught here is not God's final word, even in the Old Testament, about divorce. Malachi 2:16 condemns divorce in the strongest of terms. Many have tried to say that God didn't actually "hate" divorce, but that is what the text says. The New Testament texts (Mt 5:31-32; 19:7-9; Mk 10:4-12; Lk 16:18; 1 Cor 7:10-11) make the same point, permitting divorce only in the cases of irreconcilable adultery and unalterable abandonment.

When Jesus was questioned about this passage in Mark 10:2-12 and Matthew 19:1-9, he explained to the Pharisees that Moses had recorded this word "because of the hardness of your hearts," but the principles of Genesis 2:24 were still normative for all marriage. The two were to become one flesh. What God had joined together, no person was to separate.

Deuteronomy 24:1-4, however, deals only with the situation in which a former partner wishes to return to a previous marriage partner after one or the other has been married to a different person in the meantime and then divorced. There are three reasons the first husband, then, could not take back his wife after she had married another: (1) "she has been defiled," (2) remarriage "would be detestable in the eyes of the LORD," and (3) it would "bring sin upon the land." The logic here is the same as that found in the incest laws of Leviticus 18 and 20. Remarrying a woman one had divorced would be like marrying one's closest relative, for that is what she had become by virtue of being of one flesh. Because the husband and wife are "one flesh" (Gen 2:24), to be physically intimate with one partner was equivalent to exposing the other half of that marriage team who was not present in the illicit sexual relationships (Lev 18:6-20).

In Hebrew thinking, marriage made the bride not just a daughter-in-law, but a daughter of her husband's parents (see Ruth 1:11; 3:1). She became a sister to her husband's brother.

The results of our investigation are the following. The main clause and actual prohibition are found in verse 4 of Deuteronomy 24. The certificate or bill of divorce was for the woman's protection (against an on-again, off-again marriage) rather than the salving of the divorcing husband's conscience. And what the "something indecent" means matters little, since it was based not on Scripture and divine principle, but on common law and the custom of the day. For example, the most recent attempt to define "something indecent" views it as a euphemism for menstrual irregularities that would render a woman perpetually unclean and thus prohibit her from intercourse (Lev 15:14). Such a condition created a convenient excuse for the first husband to get out of a marriage not to his liking.[1]

Note

[1]See John Walton, *Hebrew Studies* 32 (1991): 7-17.

Children Shall Not Be Put to Death for Their Fathers' Sins

Fathers shall not be put to death for their children,
nor children put to death for their fathers;
each is to die for his own sin.
DEUTERONOMY 24:16

The principle governing Israelite courts was that human governments must not impute to children or grandchildren the guilt that their fathers or forebears accumulated. In Scripture each person stands before God as accountable for his or her own sin.

While this principle is acknowledged in Deuteronomy 24:16, there seem to be cases where it was not put in practice. For example, the child born to David and Bathsheba died because of their sin (2 Sam 12:14-18). And Saul's seven grandchildren were put to death because of Saul's sin (2 Sam 21:5-9). How are we to reconcile these contradictory sets of facts?

Some will also bring up the fact that the sins of the fathers have an ill effect on the children to the third and fourth generations (Ex 20:5; Deut 5:9). Surely this is a direct contradiction of the principle in Deuteronomy 24:16.

But Deuteronomy 24:16 is dealing with normal criminal law. It explicitly forbids blaming the children for the sin and guilt earned by the parent. If the son deserves the death penalty, the father must not be put to death in his place, or vice versa. This point is repeated in a number of texts, such as 2 Kings 14:6; 2 Chronicles 25:4; Jeremiah 31:30; and Ezekiel 18:20.

The legal principle of dealing with each individual according to individual guilt is one side of the equation. The other side is that God has reserved for himself the right to render all final decisions. Not all situations can, or are, resolved in human courts. Some must await the verdict that God will give.

There is a third element that must be accounted for as well. This notion is difficult for Westerners to appreciate, since we place such a high premium on the individual. But Scripture warns us that there is such a thing as corporate responsibility. None of us functions in complete isolation from the society and neighborhood to which we are attached. Lines of affinity reach beyond our home and church groups to whole communities and eventually to our nation and the world in which we live.

There are three factors involved in communal responsibility in the Old Testament. First is *unity*. Often the whole group is treated as a single unit. In 1 Samuel 5:10-11, for example, the ark of God came to Ekron of the Philistines. Because the bubonic plague had broken out in the previous Philistine cities where the ark had been taken, the Ekronites cried out, "They have brought the ark of the god of Israel around to us to kill us and our people." The whole group sensed that they would share in the guilt of what their leaders had done in capturing the ark of God.

Second, sometimes a single figure *represents* the whole group. Rather than someone who embodies the psychology of the group, this is a case of one, such as the suffering Servant of the

Lord, standing in for many others.

The third factor is *oscillation* from the individual to the group, and vice versa. The classic example appears in Joshua 7:11, where the Lord affirms, "Israel has sinned," even though Achan confesses, "I have sinned" (Josh 7:20).

Each situation must be evaluated to see whether it is a principle of a human court that is involved, a divine prerogative of final judgment or a case of corporate solidarity. We in the West still understand that one traitor can imperil a whole army, but we do not always understand how individual actions carry over into the divine arena or have widespread implications. Scripture works with all three simultaneously.

In the case of David and Bathsheba, it is clear that the loss of the baby was linked to the fact that David committed adultery with Uriah's wife, though Uriah remained determined to serve David faithfully in battle. This did not involve a human court but was a matter of divine prerogative.

The story about Saul's seven grandchildren takes us into the area of national guilt. Saul violated a treaty made with the Gibeonites in the name of the Lord (Josh 9:3-15). The whole nation was bound by this treaty made in Joshua's day. Thus when Saul, as head of the nation, committed this atrocity against the Gibeonites, it was an act against God and an act that involved the whole nation. A divinely initiated famine devastated the land until the demands of justice were met. When David inquired into the reason for the famine, God answered, "It is on account of Saul and his blood-stained house; it is because he put the Gibeonites to death" (2 Sam 21:1).

Saul and his sons had already fallen in the battle at Mount Gilboa, but his household shared in the stigma. Only God knew why the seven grandchildren shared in the guilt; it is not spelled out in the text. Apparently they had had some degree of complicity in the matter. Because only God knew, it was up to God, not a human court, to settle such cases.

As for the commandment that has the sins of the fathers visiting the children to the third and fourth generations, we can only observe that the text clearly teaches that this happens when the children repeat the motivating cause of their parents' sin— that is, they too hate God. But when the children love God, the effect is lovingkindness for thousands of generations!

Both individual responsibility and group or communal responsibility are taught in Scripture. We must carefully define and distinguish these types of responsibility. But in no case should the principle of courts be to blame children for the wrongful deeds of their forebears. And if God demanded that principle as a basis for fairness in human governments, should we think he would do any less in the running of his own government?

No one will ever be denied eternal life because of what his or her forebears did or did not do. Each will live eternally or suffer everlasting judgment for his or her own actions (Ezek 18). Our standard of what constitutes fairness and justice, after all, is rooted in the character of God himself.

· CHAPTER 26 ·

Achan Took the Devoted Things; Thus Israel Sinned

But the Israelites acted unfaithfully in regard to the devoted things;
Achan . . . took some of them. So the LORD'S anger
burned against Israel. . . .
The LORD said to Joshua, ". . . Israel has sinned; they have violated
my covenant, which I commanded them to keep. They have taken
some of the devoted things; they have stolen, they have lied,
they have put them with their own possessions."
JOSHUA 7:1, 10-11

It is not clear from the first verse of Joshua 7 whether the whole nation
was unfaithful or just one man, Achan. But if it was only one
man who sinned, as the story later discloses, why was the trans-
gression imputed to the whole nation? It would appear that
Achan alone should have been punished on the principle that
"the soul who sins is the one who will die" (Ezek 18:4).

Another troubling feature in this text is the identification of
the "devoted things." What were they, and why should their
possession jeopardize the Israelites' mission of attacking Ai?

The best way to begin is to start with the question of the "devoted things." This is a very distinctive concept in the Old Testament. The word used, *herem*, means the "curse" or, more accurately, the "thing dedicated for destruction." This word comes from the verb "to separate"; hence the Arabic word *harem*, meaning an enclosure set aside for the king or prince's women. In many ways, the act of dedicating *herem* is the reverse of the voluntary dedication spoken of in Romans 12:1-2. Both are acts of separating oneself or something unto God. But in the case of *herem*, the placing of an item under "the ban," or its dedication "to destruction," is an involuntary act, whereas what is "holy" to the Lord is separated unto him as a voluntary act.

Behind this concept lies the fact that all the earth belongs to the Lord and all that is in it. After mortals had tried the patience of God to the limit, he finally stepped in and required that what he owned should come back to him. The judgment of fire and death meant that all life and all gifts returned to the Lord, their owner. Items that could not burn, such as silver, gold and certain metals, were declared to belong to the Lord. They were to be placed in the tabernacle or temple of God. They had been set apart for destruction and hence were sacred.

Under no circumstances could these items be sold, collected or redeemed by substituting something else for them. There was a compulsory dedication connected with them. Jericho was one of the few places to be placed under this "curse" or "ban" in the Old Testament (Josh 6:21). Other such cities included Ai (Josh 8:26), Makkedah (Josh 10:28) and Hazor (Josh 11:11).

Interestingly, the word *herem* is the last word in the Old Testament canon (in English order). Malachi 4:6 warns that God might come and take a "forced dedication" if men and women persist in refusing to give a voluntary one.

Perhaps it will be seen, now, why Achan's sin was viewed with such severity. He had done more than take several battle me-

mentos; he had robbed God of items that specifically indicated that he was the Lord of the whole earth and should have received praise and honor from the Canaanites of Jericho.

Make no mistake: Achan was responsible for his own sin. Whether other members of his family were participants in the crime cannot be determined for certain, though it seems likely. Joshua 7:24 tells us that "his sons and daughters, his cattle, donkeys and sheep, his tent and all that he had" were brought to the Valley of Achor ("trouble"), and there "all Israel stoned him" (v. 25). While the text begins by focusing on Achan, saying they "stoned *him*," it continues noting that "they burned *them*" and "they stoned *them*." Thus it would appear that the children were accomplices to the crime.

Since Achan had violated the ban and brought the goods from Jericho into his tent, he in essence made his tent, its contents and whatever was under the aegis of that tent part of the destruction and judgment that was on Jericho.

Finally, we must ask why the whole nation was viewed by God as an organic unity. Can the sin of one member of the nation or group defile everyone?

That is exactly the point made by this text. It is not difficult to see how the goodness of one person can bring blessing on the whole group. God blessed the whole world through Abraham (Gen 12:3). And we rarely complain when we enjoy the blessing and accumulated goodness of God upon our nation as a result of the godly lives of our ancestors.

But it seems an entirely different matter when the curses of the one are passed down to his or her descendants. How can this teaching be squared with Deuteronomy 24:16—"Fathers shall not be put to death for their children, nor children put to death for their fathers: each is to die for his own sin"?

Deuteronomy 24:16 is a principle for human courts to use in assigning the death penalty; it is not meant to deny divine judgment for just cause or to invalidate corporate responsibility. In a real sense, our acts do have ramifications beyond our own fortunes and future. The act of one traitor can imperil a battalion of soldiers, a nation or a multinational corporation. In the same way, one thoughtless act of a member of a community can have enormous consequences for the whole group.

This in no way bears on the ultimate destiny and salvation of any one of the persons in that group, but it can have enormous implications for the temporal and material well-being of each member.

When an individual Israelite violated a specific command of God, it brought sin on the whole group. In that case, the sin ignited the anger of God against the whole group. Achan was not acting merely on his own behalf when he sinned. As a leader among the clans of the important tribe of Judah, he had committed sacrilege; he had stolen what God had declared to be both sacred and separated from ordinary objects. Such a crime was aimed directly at God and at his covenant. It impinged on his right to be Lord and infringed on his rights of ownership. It had to be dealt with immediately and severely, just as did the sin of Ananias and Sapphira in the New Testament (Acts 5).

God holds each person individually responsible for his or her own sin; that is clear. But some, by virtue of their position or office, their offense against that which is sacred to God, or the implications that their acts have for their group, can also bring the wrath of God on their nation, community, institution or group. There are times where we are our nation's keepers. When we deny or ignore this reality, Western individualism runs amuck and biblical truth is neglected.

· C H A P T E R 2 7 ·

The Gibeonites Deceived Joshua, but He Could Not Touch Them

Joshua asked, "Who are you and where do you come from?"
They answered: "Your servants have come from a very distant country
because of the fame of the LORD your God." . . . Three days after they
made the treaty with the Gibeonites, the Israelites heard that they
were neighbors, living near them. . . . The whole assembly grumbled
against the leaders, but all the leaders answered, "We have given
them our oath by the LORD, the God of Israel,
and we cannot touch them now."
JOSHUA 9:8-9, 16, 18-19

The story of the ruse pulled by the Gibeonites presents several moral and ethical dilemmas. Is a person required to keep his or her word when the means used to obtain that promise were obviously false? Can the end justify the means in cases such as the one before us? Do wartime conditions lessen the requirements for keeping one's word?

Why did Joshua feel that he was obligated to maintain the terms of a treaty into which he had been tricked? Could he not have legitimately said that he was involved in a war and the enemy remained just that, regardless of the agreement they had reached? Why did Joshua act so faintheartedly for a military general?

The Gibeonites were worried after they had witnessed the sudden fall of Jericho and Ai. The citizens of Gibeon and its associated cities, seized with alarm, decided that they would approach the invading armies of Joshua and pretend that they had come from a distant country and wanted to make a treaty. The delegation dressed themselves in torn clothing and sandals, and carried awkwardly mended wineskins. Even their bread was crumbly and dry. They played their parts to perfection; Joshua and the leadership of Israel were, indeed, completely conned. The deception was masterfully carried out.

Three days after the treaty had been ratified by oath, it was learned that these were men from Gibeon and its environs. That city was only six miles northwest of Jerusalem. Humiliated by the deception, the Israelite people grumbled about the way the leadership had mishandled this matter.

Why the Gibeonites had chosen to risk so much on the Israelites' commitment to honoring their promise is difficult to explain. Had they gotten an initial indication that the God of this people required truthfulness and integrity from his own? Or did the Gibeonites share a common Semitic concept of the effect of the word—that once a word had gone forth, there was no way to stop it, for it had a mission to fulfill? But that concept seems rather lofty for the Canaanites, given what we know about their ethics and morals.

Speculation will not help fill the gaps in our knowledge. What we do know is that for Joshua the matter was now a sacred trust, since the Israelite leaders had given their oath by the name of the God of Israel. To go back on that word would be to tarnish the high name of God. For the moment, the Gibeonites had succeeded. Eventually, they would be put under a perpetual servant-hood as woodcutters and water carriers for the house of God. They would appear in this role as late as the postexilic times of Nehemiah.

It is true that the leaders should have sought God's guidance in their uncertainty. But they did not.

This story is particularly difficult for moderns to understand, for we do not generally have the same concept of the effect of one's words. In Old Testament times, giving one's word was not taken lightly. Once a word was uttered, it could not be flippantly recalled or canceled. God saw to it that each word had the effect for which it was intended. This is not to say that a magical view of words is taught in the Old Testament, or that there is an independent power in words. The health-wealth-and-prosperity gospel that would urge us to simply "name it [our desire] and claim it" has been exploded as being nonbiblical.

There was, however, a sacredness to the word uttered in the Lord's name. Integrity demanded that such a word be kept, for it had been sealed with an oath.

Truth-telling and integrity in keeping one's word were serious matters for all who loved and obeyed the God of truth. And to make a covenant in God's name was binding, for it meant that God's reputation was involved. True, the grounds and means the Gibeonites used to obtain this treaty or covenant were less than honorable, but that in no way nullified the terms of the agreement, once it had been agreed to in the great name of the God of heaven and earth.

· C H A P T E R 28 ·

The Sun Stood Still and the Moon Stopped

On the day the LORD gave the Amorites over to Israel,
Joshua said to the LORD in the presence of Israel:
"O sun, stand still over Gibeon,
O moon, over the Valley of Aijalon."
So the sun stood still,
and the moon stopped,
till the nation avenged itself on its enemies,
as it is written in the Book of Jashar.
The sun stopped in the middle of the sky and delayed going down
about a full day. There has never been a day like it before or since,
a day when the LORD listened to a man.
Surely the LORD was fighting for Israel!
JOSHUA 10:12-14

Among the many miracles recorded in the Bible, this one is perhaps the most notable. Did the Lord actually halt the earth's rotation for a period of approximately twenty-four hours, so that the sun stood still in the sky and the moon failed to come up at its appointed time? And if God did halt the earth's normal rotation for a full day, would this not have led to an inconceivable catastrophe for the entire planet and everything that is held on its surface by the force of gravity? The implications of some of these questions are, indeed, cosmic.

Or is there some other meaning to the natural force of the words used in this account? For example, can the words in verse 13 (literally rendered: "The sun did not hasten to go down for about a whole day") point to a retardation of the earth's movement, so that it took forty-eight hours rather than twenty-four hours for the earth to make its circuit around the sun? Or could the Hebrew word *dom*, "stand still" (much like our onomatopoeic word "be dumb") signify that the sun was to remain hidden— hence "silent"—during the violent thunderstorm that accompanied the troops as they fled before the Israelites down the Valley of Aijalon? These are some of the reasons this passage is listed among our "hard sayings."

Of course, the God who made the universe can momentarily stop it without the catastrophes that most of us would envisage according to the laws known to us at this time. Surely he is capable of holding in abeyance those physical laws that might have countermanded his actions with regard to the sun and the moon. But the question is, *Would* he have done so? This is like saying that only God is omnipotent. Yet God will not do contradictory things like make ropes with only one end or squares in the form of circles; and he will never sin. There are some things that he will not do because they are contradictory to his very nature. The question then is, would stopping the planet be such a contradiction? Most would say that it is.

Alleged stories about a long day in Egyptian, Chinese and Hindu sources are difficult to validate. Similarly, the reports that some astronomers, and more recently some space scientists, have uncovered evidence for a missing day are difficult to vouch for. The claim by Edward Charles Pickering of the Harvard Observatory and Professor Totten of Yale that they had discovered a day missing from the annals of the heavens has never been sub-stantiated, since no records exist to support it. It has been said in defense of this omission that the university officials preferred not to keep records of that sort in their archives. But that has not been demonstrated either. Some other explanation is needed.

What happened on that day when Joshua was pursuing the Amorites after a long night's forced march from Gilgal, a city near Jericho? That day the army covered more than thirty miles over some pretty rough terrain. The enemy fled westward to Beth Horon and then turned south into the Valley of Aijalon ("Deerfield"). At that point, the men, having made an all-night up-hill climb from Gilgal, were exhausted. The heat of the July day was sapping what little energy they had left. But to their great relief, God sent a hailstorm that kept pace with the forward ranks of the fleeing Amorites. More were dying that day from the Lord's hailstones than from the Israelites' arrows and spears. The Lord had heard the prayer of his leader Joshua and answered in a most dramatic way.

Given the presence of a hailstorm (v. 11), it is difficult to see how the sun could have been seen as stopped in the sky. There was light under the cloud cover, of course, but there would have been no actual view of the sun during a hailstorm so violent that it was killing the Amorites by the scores.

We can conclude that *dom* in verse 13 should be translated "was dumb" or "silent." The sun did not "stop" in the middle of the sky, but its burning heat was "silenced." The presence of the hailstorm lends more than a little credence to this view. In a sense, then, this is not "Joshua's long day" but rather "Joshua's long night," for the coolness brought by the storm relieved the men and permitted them to go on fighting and marching for a total of more than eighteen hours. This seems to be the prefer-able interpretation.

Some have suggested that there was a prolongation of the day merely in the sense that the men did in one day what should have taken them two. But this suggestion fails to account for some of the special vocabulary used in this text.

Others have argued that God produced an optical prolongation of the sunshine, continuing its effect far beyond the normal time of sunset. Perhaps there was an unusual refraction of the sun's rays, or perhaps a comet or meteorite appeared in the heavens just about this time. Both of these ideas, however, do not account for enough time, for usually these types of astronomical events are of short duration.

The best solution is this. Joshua prayed early in the morning, while the moon was in the western sky and the sun was in the east, that God would intervene on their behalf. God answered Joshua and sent a hailstorm. This had the effect of prolonging the darkness and shielding the men from the searing rays of the summer sun. The sun, therefore, was "silenced" in the middle of the sky, and the moon "did not hasten" to come.

What a day to remember, for on it God went out and personally fought for Israel—and more died from the hailstones than from the weapons of the army of Israel!

If There Is Dew Only on the Fleece, Then I Will Know

*Gideon said to God, "If you will save Israel by my hand
as you have promised—look, I will place a wool fleece on the threshing
floor. If there is dew only on the fleece and all the ground is dry,
then I will know that you will save Israel by my hand, as you said."
And that is what happened. . . . Then Gideon said to God,
"Do not be angry with me. Let me make just one more request.
Allow me one more test with the fleece. This time make the fleece dry
and the ground covered with dew." That night God did so.
Only the fleece was dry; all the ground was covered with dew.*
JUDGES 6:36-40

Was Gideon wrong, as some say, in asking God for reassurance by means of a wet or dry fleece? Had not God made his will clear to Gideon already at the time of his call (Judg 6:14-16)? While it is understandable that Gideon was apprehensive over his impending conflict with Midian, given the disparity in the number of weapons, number of men and morale of the soldiers, he was still wrong in doubting God. Or, at least, that is what some contend.

Did Gideon use a proper type of test? Supposing a test *is* permissible, isn't it wrong to ask God to accommodate our weakness, to assure us through physical signs of a word he has already spoken?

One further objection focuses on the fact that Gideon did not keep his word. Gideon promised that he would know God was going to use him to deliver Israel if God made the fleece wet and left the ground dry. Though God complied, Gideon went back on his word and insisted on running the same experiment in reverse fashion before he would believe. So what can we say, not only for Gideon but also to modern believers who wish to use similar tactics in order to validate the will of the Lord for them?

Some who object to Gideon's method for discerning God's will feel that he was not really desiring to know the will of God. Instead, they say, Gideon was angling to have that will *changed!*

This does not appear to be the case, based on what we are told in the text itself. Such an assertion tends to psychologize Gideon. How can we penetrate into his heart and mind and say what it was that Gideon was feeling or hoping?

Clearly, Gideon struggled. But he wanted God to provide his overwhelmed mind with more evidence for the word "as [God had] said" (v. 37). He *was* responding to God's call (vv. 14-16). Thus he was hesitant, but not unbelieving.

What about the matter of asking for signs? When we do so, are we acting like the scribes and Pharisees of Jesus' day, who always wanted a sign? And how specific is the will of God in our ordinary life? Granted: in revelation God often gave specific, detailed instructions for particular actions. But is Judges 6 an invitation for all believers to demand similar specificity? Must the will of God be a dot with a fixed point and nothing else?

Gideon's boldness can be seen both in his asking for a sign and in his specifying what that sign should be. The sign, though simple, involved a miracle. He would place the fleece on the leveled ground where the people threshed their grain (probably in the entrance to the city gate). If the dew was on the fleece alone while all the ground was dry, then he would know that God really would use him to deliver Israel from the hand of the Midianites.

The next night, using rather deferential language, he asked that the sign be reversed, with the fleece being dry and the ground soaked with the dew of the night. In both instances Gideon's request was granted, confirming what God had promised—that his strength comes to peak performance and full throttle in our weakness (2 Cor 12:9).

Thus Gideon's faith was supported. The phantom fears that had haunted his countrymen about the Midianites no longer afflicted him. Before setting out to overthrow the Midianites, he had approached God in prayer, and there he had found his courage renewed and fortified. His importunity was not wrong. And actually he provides a model for us: when we are beset by internal struggles and when challenges seem too great for us to handle, we must go to God in prayer.

Nevertheless, this passage does not give encouragement to those who assume they can expect God to attend each of his instructions with whatever signs we may request! God could just as well have refused Gideon's request. The fact that he didn't does not set a precedent to which any and all believers may appeal in their moment of distress. God may be pleased to repeat such an act of mercy, but he is not bound to satisfy our desire for visual, physical miracles to confirm his will. Whether he does so rests in his hand alone.

Samson Marries an Unbelieving Philistine

When [Samson] returned, he said to his father and mother,
"I have seen a Philistine woman in Timnah; now get her for me as my wife."
His father and mother replied, "Isn't there an acceptable woman among
your relatives or among all our people? Must you go to the uncircumcised
Philistines to get a wife?" But Samson said to his father, "Get her
for me. She's the right one for me." (His parents did not know
that this was from the LORD, who was seeking an occasion to confront
the Philistines; for at that time they were ruling over Israel.)
JUDGES 14:2-4

God had clearly forbidden the Israelites to intermarry with the Canaanites (Ex 34:11-16; Deut 7:1-4). The Philistines, not technically listed as Canaanites, were actually cousins to the Egyptians (Gen 10:14). Nevertheless, it would seem that the principle of avoiding intermarriage would apply to the Philistines as well as the Canaanites, since the rule was based not on race but on religion. Believers were not to marry unbelievers.

Furthermore, there is an ambiguity in verse 4. Who sought the occasion against the Philistines: God or Samson? The Hebrew text simply says "he." Some commentators, such as George Bush, J. K. F. Keil and Andrew Robert Fausset, take Samson as the intended reference; others such as Dale Ralph Davis, Leon Wood and Luke Wiseman make God the antecedent of "he was seeking . . ."

The story of Samson serves as the thematic climax to the book of Judges. The refrain of the book is "everyone did as he saw fit," or "did what was right in his own eyes" (Judg 17:6; 21:25). The narrator of Judges uses the same refrain to describe Samson in chapter 14. A literal translation of verse 3 would render his demand thus: "Get her for me, for she is right in my eyes." Again, Judges 14:7 comments, "She was right in Samson's eyes" (NIV "he liked her"). In this respect, Samson was typical of his period of Israelite history—it was the day for doing one's own thing.

It is probably best to assume that the antecedent of "who" or "he" in verse 4 is meant to be Yahweh, since to think otherwise would strain grammatical construction. Samson appears to be governed more by his glands than by any secret purpose on behalf of his nation. He was doing his own thing. The purpose was not his but God's.

But that will only seem to make the difficulty of this passage worse. How could the Lord go back on his own rules in order to accomplish some other goal, even a high purpose?

James B. Jordan cuts the Gordian knot first by agreeing that God was guiding Samson to move toward marriage, even though Samson was doing his own thing. The purpose of such a marriage, in Jordan's view, was evangelism. Had the nation of Philistia accepted the olive branch symbolized by this marriage and recognized that they were occupying Israel's land, the war would have ended. But instead, the riddle Samson put forth at the banquet (14:10-20) allowed the Philistines' true colors to show. Most of the Israelites had failed to see the domination of the Philistines for what it was; they needed to be stirred up. Since the Philistines were cousins to the Egyptians, the captivity of Israel to the Philistines was equivalent to captivity in Egypt. The lionlike Sphinx is the guardian of Egypt, and it was a lion that attacked Samson as he went down to Philistia.

Now all of this is just a bit too rich for my blood! Jordan's argument depends too much on symbolism—especially given that a particularly difficult theological issue has been raised. His solution seems contrived when judged from the standpoint of an outsider.

Better is the approach of Dale Ralph Davis. For him, the one who was seeking an occasion against the Philistines was Yahweh. But that does not mean God condoned everything Samson did or the way he did it. Says Davis, "Many Christian parents have stood in the sandals of Manoah and his wife. They have, though realizing their own sinful inadequacies, faithfully taught, prayed for, disciplined, and loved a son or a daughter only to see that child willfully turn from the way of the Lord. No one can deny it is anything but devastating. Yet one should not forget verse 4: 'But his father and mother did not realize it was from Yahweh.' What we don't know may yet prove to be our deepest comfort."[1]

The sin of Samson must not be attributed to the Lord; but the deliverance of the Israelites by Samson was from the Lord. Remember, scriptural language frequently attributes directly to God what he merely permits.

Samson surely was directed by God to seek an occasion against the Philistines and to lead the Israelites in breaking out from under their yoke. But Samson did not take the time to inquire of the Lord how, or in what legitimate ways, he might do this. We do not find him asking, as his successor Samuel did, "Speak, Lord, for your servant is listening." Nor did he seek divine guidance when his parents questioned his seeking a bride among the

Philistines. All that mattered was whether he was pleased—whether his choice was "right in his own eyes." Little wonder, then, that he would only *begin* to deliver Israel from the Philistines. Perhaps his potential for greatness was truncated by his vices, his partaking too deeply of the cultural appetites of his day.

Our conclusion is that Samson was neither directed nor tempted by God to do what God had specifically prohibited in his Word. God wanted the defeat of the Philistines, but that did not give Samson carte blanche. Moreover, God's blessing on one or more aspects of a person's life is no indication that everything that person does is approved. Samson was plain bullheaded about this decision, and he refused to listen to his parents or to God. But neither Samson's foolishness nor his stubbornness would prevent the design of God from being fulfilled.

Note

[1]Dale Ralph Davis, *Such a Great Salvation* (Grand Rapids: Baker, 1990), p. 172.

A Mother
Curses a Thief
Then Blesses Him

*Now a man named Micah from the hill country of Ephraim
said to his mother, "The eleven hundred shekels of silver
that were taken from you and about which I heard you utter a curse—
I have that silver with me; I took it." Then his mother said,
"The LORD bless you, my son!"*
JUDGES 17:1-2

Here is a story that seems so mixed up and crazy that it easily raises
as much embarrassment as anything else. What is happening in
this densely packed exchange between mother and son?

One wonders where the writer's—or even God's—evaluation
of things appears in this bizarre narrative. How can a mother
curse a thief and then turn around and bless him when she finds
out the culprit was her own son? Isn't thievery still wrong for
all the Bible and its people? And how can God suddenly bless
what was just cursed? What did the woman expect to happen?
Why did she utter such a strange response upon learning that
her money was in the hands of one of her own children?

The writer of the book of Judges wanted us to see that everything was out of control in Israel. Almost every aspect of this
story discloses a violation of the will of God as he had revealed
it to Israel.

Clearly the narrative is compressed and in a tightly woven
form. Micah's mother, realizing that she had been swindled out
of eleven hundred shekels of silver, responded with an oath. The
effect of such an oath was not taken lightly in that culture, for
once the word was uttered, it was as if it were an accomplished
fact. It was not, as it often is in our culture, where someone
might say something off the cuff and then quickly, or even later,
retrieve it: "Aw, forget I said that; I didn't mean anything by it."
The Israelites of Old Testament times believed that God mon-
itored all speech and saw to it that vows, oaths and even idle
words fulfilled their mission. Theirs was not a magical view of
words; but they did know that talk is not cheap and words often
carry consequences.

When Micah heard his mother cut loose with this oath, he
immediately confessed that he was the thief. He obviously feared
the consequences of his mother's oath. It is doubtful that his
mother had suspected her son and spoken her curse in his hearing deliberately. Probably she had been unaware of her son's
presence. Curses were taken too seriously in those days for us
to think otherwise.

Delighted to have the money back, the mother was not immediately concerned to ask Micah why he had stolen. On the contrary, she was now worried about reversing the effect of the
curse she had invoked over her son's head. That is why she said,
"The LORD bless you, my son." She hoped that this blessing
would mitigate, if not nullify, the negative effect of the curse
placed on Micah.

Now it must be made clear that the Bible only reports what
happened here; it does not teach that any of this is normative or

worth emulating. The narrative must be read in the context of the revelation of God up to this point.

At least six sins can be discovered in this story. First, the eighth commandment (Ex 20:15) is clear: "You shall not steal." Micah stole from his mother, and later the tribe of Dan stole his religious articles from his private sanctuary.

In the second place, Micah and his mother, wishing to buy some insurance, as it were, against God's carrying out her original oath, gave part of the money for the making of several images. This ran counter to the second commandment. But notice how dulled their theological senses were. How could they have expected God's blessing when they had substituted graven and molten images for the sovereign Lord of the universe?

Third, Micah established a private sanctuary in his home. God had said there was to be only one sanctuary for all the people, and that was at the tabernacle in Shiloh (Deut 12:4-14). God had promised to dwell there and place his name in a central sanctuary, not in individual tents or homes throughout Israel.

Then Micah made one of his sons his private priest, though God had said that only members of the family of Aaron in the tribe of Levi were to represent the people before the altar. Apparently that arrangement did not work out, and Micah then hired a Levite who had been wandering the countryside looking for work. Here again, Micah (and later the tribe of Dan) were still in violation of God's directive, for Aaron and his family were the sole legitimate priests.

When the tribe of Dan decided to leave the coastal plain, they committed the fifth sin in this narrative, by moving from their allotted inheritance. They should have conquered the territory assigned to them rather than capitulating to the Philistines and moving north to the exposed city of Laish.

Finally, the movement of the Levite from his assigned city to work for Micah and then for the tribe of Dan shows that he was

an opportunist. As a Levite, he would have had an assigned place
to work. Instead of remaining there, he determined to make his
own way in the world; as a result a number of people were
impacted by his sin.

Neither the story nor the times are pretty; but this account is
entirely realistic, and its implied warning is instructive. We
should not doubt in the darkness what God has already told us
in the light.

Ruth Uncovered Boaz's Feet and Lay Down

*When Boaz had finished eating and drinking and was in
good spirits, he went over to lie down at the far end of the grain pile.
Ruth approached quietly, uncovered his feet and lay down.
In the middle of the night something startled the man, and he turned
and discovered a woman lying at his feet. "Who are you?" he asked.
"I am your servant Ruth," she said. "Spread the corner of
your garment over me, since you are a kinsman-redeemer."*
RUTH 3:7-9

Some readers of and commentators on this text have suggested that
Ruth's bold move that night on the threshing floor went beyond
the normal boundaries of propriety and included sexual relations
with Boaz.

The argument for such a reading goes like this. Harvest time
the world over is a time of celebration of the rites of fertility. At
these times, the ancients allowed themselves more license than
usual. During this harvest celebration, then, after Boaz had im-
bibed enough wine to make himself drunk, Ruth made her move

in order to force him into marriage.

Others have interpreted Boaz's "feet" as a sexual euphemism for the male reproductive organ. If this were the meaning, then the story would be making a discreet reference to fleshly indulgence.

Both of these suggestions are wide of the mark and without support in this text, for actually the biblical writer chose his words carefully so as to avoid any possible innuendo.

To begin with, it is extremely unlikely that Boaz was drunk after the good meal he had eaten. The text simply says that he "was in good spirits." His mood was mellow, and his demeanor was upbeat. And why not? He had the results of all his hard labors right there on the threshing floor with him. But his feasting brought on drowsiness, so he retired to one side of the pile of grain that had been threshed. It is doubtful that he would have guarded this pile of grain by himself, that there would have been no other workers present who would awaken at the crack of dawn to get back to work alongside him.

Later, after Boaz had fallen asleep, Ruth went and carefully uncovered his feet and apparently crawled under his cover, lying perpendicular to his feet. There are no sexual overtones in the reference to his feet, for Boaz was startled at midnight when his feet suddenly touched the woman's body.

Ruth immediately made her objective clear when she requested, "Spread the corner of your garment over me." She was using the accepted idiom meaning "Marry me"—other passages in which the same expression is used are Ezekiel 16:8, Deuteronomy 22:30 and 27:20, and Malachi 2:16. No doubt the idiom reflected the custom, still practiced by some Arabs, of a man's throwing a garment over the woman he has decided to take as his wife. The gesture is a symbol of protection as well as a declaration that the man is willing to enter into sexual consummation with his chosen partner.

Boaz had prayed in Ruth 2:12 that Ruth might be rewarded by the Lord under whose wings she had taken refuge. Ruth now essentially asked Boaz to answer his own prayer, for "garment-cover" and "wing" are from a similar root in Hebrew.

Ruth's reason for this action is expressed in her appeal to Boaz as a "kinsman-redeemer." That is a legal status. Under Jewish law, then, her request was not particularly unusual.

That Boaz handled himself honorably can be seen in his revelation that there was someone who actually had prior claim over Ruth and her inheritance, since he was a closer relative. However, if he should prove unwilling to take responsibility in the matter (and he was not), then Boaz would marry Ruth.

Remarkably, Ruth seems willing to marry even this other relative sight unseen, again subordinating her own happiness to her duty of raising up an heir to her deceased husband and to Naomi. In doing so, she demonstrates again why this book singles her out as a most worthy example of what Proverbs 31 refers to as a "virtuous woman," or a person "of noble character."

The charges against Ruth and Boaz are false and without foundation. While the couple's encounter did occur in the context of darkness and sleep, the text does not present their behavior as morally questionable or even particularly abnormal within the social and moral conventions of the godly remnant of those days.

· C H A P T E R 3 3 ·

The Lord Said, "They Have Rejected Me as Their King"

*And the LORD told him, "Listen to all that the people
are saying to you; it is not you they have rejected, but they
have rejected me as their king." . . . But the people refused
to listen to Samuel. "No!" they said. "We want a king over us.
Then we will be like all the other nations, with a king to lead us
and to go out before us and fight our battles." When Samuel heard
all that the people said, he repeated it before the LORD.
The LORD answered, "Listen to them and give them a king."*
1 SAMUEL 8:7, 19-22

What makes this section one of our hard sayings is not the fact that
it contains what some have unfairly labeled the ramblings of a
disappointed prophet. Instead, it is the fact that up until very
recent times, most nonevangelical Old Testament scholars
strongly believed that they detected an ambivalent attitude toward kingship in the narratives of 1 Samuel 8—12, in light of the
covenantal tone of 1 Samuel 11:14—12:25.

It has been fairly common to find 1 Samuel 8—12 character-

ized as a collection of independent story units or tradition com-
plexes, some being promonarchial and others antimonarchial.
This division was supposedly evidenced in different attitudes and
responses to the idea of a monarchy and kingship in Israel.
Generally an antimonarchial orientation was attributed to 1
Samuel 8, 10:17-27 and 12, while a promonarchial stance was seen
in 1 Samuel 9:1—10:16 and 11. Endorsing this analysis of the
material would leave us with a dilemma: how could Scripture
both approve and reprove the concept of a monarchy?

A second problem in the debate surrounding 1 Samuel 8—12
was the sequencing of events presented in the book. It has been
widely alleged that the present sequence is an artificial device
imposed by a late editor as a result of the growth of tradition.

Finally, many scholars have said that the antimonarchial sections (1 Sam 8; 10:17-27; 12) show indications of editorial revisions arising from Deuteronomic influence; this argument is
based on a late dating of Deuteronomy in the postexilic period
of the fifth and fourth century B.C.

Each of these three allegations must be answered. There is no
doubt that a tension of sorts does exist in the narratives of 1
Samuel 8—12. The prospect of establishing a kingship in Israel
elicited numerous reservations, and these are fairly aired in 1
Samuel 8, 10:17-27 and 12.

Yet it cannot be forgotten that kingship was also within the
direct plan and permission of God. God had divulged that part
of his plan as far back as the days of Moses (Deut 17:14-20).
Accordingly, when Samuel presented Saul to the people, it was
as the one whom the Lord had chosen (1 Sam 10:24). Saul's
appointment was the outcome of the twice-repeated guidance
that Samuel received, "Listen to all that the people are saying"
(1 Sam 8:7, 22). In fact, 1 Samuel 12:13 specifically says, "See, the
LORD has set a king over you."

But here is the important point. These five chapters of 1 Samuel cannot be neatly divided into two contrasting sets of narratives; the ambivalence is present even *within* the units that have been labeled as corresponding to one side or the other! The problem, in fact, is to explain this ambivalence at all. What is the cause for this love-hate attitude toward kingship in Israel?

My answer is the same as Robert Vannoy's.[1] It is the covenantal relationship expressed in 1 Samuel 11:14—12:25 that explains this ambivalence. The issue, then, is not the presence of kingship so much as it is the *kind* of kingship and the *reasons* for wanting a monarchy.

There is no question but that the presence of a king in Israel was fully compatible with Yahweh's covenant with Israel. What hurt Samuel and the Lord was the people's improper motive for requesting a king in the first place: they wanted to "be like all the other nations" (8:20) and have a king to lead them when they went out to fight. This was tantamount to breaking the covenant and rejecting Yahweh as their Sovereign (8:7; 10:19). To act in this manner was to forget God's provision for them in the past. Hadn't he protected them and gone before them in battle many times?

Since the people were so thoughtless in their motivation for desiring a king, it was necessary to warn them about "the manner of the king" (literal translation of *mishpat hammelek*—8:11). If what the people wanted was a contemporaneous form of monarchy, then they had better get used to all the abuses and problems of kingship as well as its splendor.

Five serious problems with the contemporary forms of kingship are cited in 1 Samuel 8:11-18. That these issues were real can be attested by roughly contemporaneous documents from Alalakh and Ugarit.[2] The problems they would experience would include a military draft (vv. 11-12), the servitude of the populace (v. 13), widespread royal confiscation of private property (v. 14), taxation (v. 15) and loss of personal liberty (vv. 16-17).

This delineation of "the manner of the king" served to define the function of kings in the Near East. But over against this was the gathering that took place at Mizpah (1 Sam 10:17-27). Here Samuel described "the manner of the kingdom" (literal translation of *mishpat hammalukah*—10:25). In so doing Samuel began to resolve the tension between Israel's improper reasons for desiring a king, their misconceptions of the king's role and function, and Yahweh's purpose in saying that he also desired Israel to have a king. Samuel's definition of "the manner of the kingdom" clearly distinguished Israelite kingship from the kingship that was practiced in the surrounding nations of that day.

In Israel, the king's role was to be compatible with Yahweh's sovereignty over the nation and also with all the laws, prescriptions and obligations of the covenant given to the people under Moses' leadership. Thus "the manner of the kingdom" was to be normative for the nation of Israel rather than "the manner of the king."

The issue of the sequencing of the narratives is less difficult. Given the tensions of the time—the various attitudes toward kingship and the legitimacy of establishing it—one can easily see how the text does reflect the back-and-forth unfolding of the process at various geographic locations and on different days. Each phase of the negotiations dramatized the seesaw nature of this battle between those holding out for the sovereignty of Yahweh and those wanting a more visible and contemporaneous model of kingship.

The most critical problem in connection with the sequencing of the events is the relationship between 1 Samuel 11:14-15 and 1 Samuel 10:17-27, particularly in connection with the statement in 11:14, "Come, let us go to Gilgal and there *reaffirm* the kingship."

This phrase constitutes the most compelling evidence for the argument that several accounts have been put together in these chapters. The simplest, and best, explanation for the meaning of this debated phrase, however, is that the reference is not to Saul, but to a renewal of allegiance to Yahweh and his covenant. It is a call for the renewal ceremony that is described in greater detail in 1 Samuel 12. This explanation makes the most sense and makes possible the best harmonization of the parallel accounts of Saul's accession to the throne in 1 Samuel 10:17-27 and 11:15.

The third and final objection concerns the alleged Deuteronomic influence on the so-called antimonarchial sections of 1 Samuel 8, 10:17-27 and 12. Bear in mind that those who raise this objection also date Deuteronomy to the fifth or fourth century B.C. rather than attributing it to Moses as it properly should be.

Their argument runs into several problems of its own. Long ago Julius Wellhausen (1844-1918) noted its basic flaw: for all of Deuteronomy's alleged antimonarchial views, it had put forth a positive "law of the king" (Deut 17:14-20) long before any of the Israelites thought of having a king! Furthermore, the pictures of David, Hezekiah and Josiah in 1 and 2 Kings (other books often alleged to be Deuteronomic in viewpoint and influence) were likewise promonarchial.

There is no doubt that Deuteronomy had a profound influence on the events described in 1 Samuel 8—12, but none of them can be shown to have resulted from a late editorializing based on an exilic or postexilic revisionist view of how kingship had come about in Israel.

Thus we conclude that none of these three problems can be used as evidence for a lack of unity, coherence or singularity of viewpoint. Most important of all, the covenantal perspective of 1 Samuel 11:14—12:25 provides the best basis for the unity and historical trustworthiness of these accounts as they presently stand in our texts.

Notes

[1]Robert Vannoy, *Covenant Renewal at Gilgal* (Cherry Hill, N.J.: Mack Publishing, 1978), p. 228.
[2]See I. Mendelson, "Samuel's Denunciation of Kingship in Light of Akkadian Documents from Ugarit," *Bulletin of the American Schools of Oriental Research* 143 (1956):17.

God Would Have Established Saul's Kingdom Forever

*"You acted foolishly," Samuel said. "You have not kept
the command the LORD your God gave you; if you had, he would
have established your kingdom over Israel for all time. But now
your kingdom will not endure; the LORD has sought out a man after
his own heart and appointed him leader of his people,
because you have not kept the LORD'S command."*
1 SAMUEL 13:13-14

How was it possible for Samuel to say that Saul's house could have had perpetuity over Israel when Genesis 49:10 had promised it to the tribe of Judah (not Benjamin, from which Saul hailed) long before Saul's reign or downfall? Of course, the Lord had planned to place a king over Israel, as Deuteronomy 17:14 had clearly taught. But if the family that was to wield the scepter was from Judah, how could God—in retrospect, to Saul's disappointment— say that Saul could indeed have been that king?

The solution to this problem is not to be found in Samuel's vacillating attitudes toward Saul, for it is clear that Saul was also

God's choice from the very beginning (1 Sam 9:16; 10:1, 24; 12:13).

The Lord had allowed the choice of the people to fall on one whose external attributes made an immediate positive impression on people. Saul's was strictly an earthly kingdom, with all the pageantry and showmanship that impress mortals.

Unfortunately, Saul was not disposed to rule in humble submission to the laws, ordinances and commandments that came from above. As one final evidence of his attitude, he had refused to wait for the appointment he had made with Samuel. As he went ahead and took over the duties of a priest, in violation of his kingly position, God decided that he would not keep his appointment with him as king.

The type of kingship Samuel had instituted under the direction of God was distinctive. It was a theocracy; the Israelite monarchy was to function under the authority and sovereignty of Yahweh himself. When this covenantal context was violated, the whole "manner of the kingdom" (1 Sam 10:25; see chapter 33 in this book) was undermined.

While this explanation may suffice for what happened in the "short haul," how shall we address the issue of God's having promised the kingship to the family of Judah, rather than the Benjamite family of Kish? Would God have actually given Saul's family a portion or all of the nation, had he listened and kept the commandments of God? Or did the writer, and hence God also, regard the two southern tribes of Judah and Benjamin as one? In that case, perhaps what had been promised to Judah could have gone to Saul just as easily as to David.

There is evidence from Scripture itself that the tribes of Benjamin and Judah were regarded as "one tribe": 1 Kings 11:36 says, "I will give one tribe to [Solomon's] son so that David my servant may always have a lamp before me in Jerusalem." If these two could later be regarded as "one," no objection can be made to doing so earlier.

Ultimately, this is one of those questions that are impossible to resolve fully, since we are asking for information that belongs to the mind of God. However, it seems important that we be able to offer several possible solutions.

Beside the notion that Benjamin and Judah may well have been regarded as one tribe, so that a Benjamite, Saul, could have fulfilled God's promise, there are several other possible, and actually preferable, suggestions.

It may well have been that God fully intended that Judah, and eventually the house of David would rule over Israel and Judah. But it's also possible that Saul's family would have been given the northern ten tribes of Israel after the division of the kingdom, which God in his omniscience of course could anticipate. That would resolve the question just as easily.

The best suggestion, however, is that God had agreed to appoint Saul king in deference to the people's deep wishes. Though the Lord had consented, this was not his directive will; he merely permitted it to happen. Eventually, what the Lord knew all along was proved true: Saul had a character flaw that precipitated his demise. Nevertheless, it is possible to describe Saul in terms of what he could have been, barring that flaw, in the kingdom of God and the kingdom of the Israelites.

A combination of these last two views is possible—that in his permissive will God would have given Saul the northern ten tribes in perpetuity without denying to the house of Judah the two southern tribes, according to his promise in Genesis 49:10. An interesting confirmation of this possibility can be seen in 1 Kings 11:38, where King Jeroboam is promised an enduring dynasty, in a parallel to the promise God had made to King David. Since the promise to Jeroboam in no way replaced the long-standing promise to the tribe of Judah and the house of David, it is similar to God's "might-have-been" to Saul. God offered the ten northern tribes to Jeroboam just as he had offered them to Saul.

One final possibility is that Saul was given a genuine, though hypothetical, promise of a perpetual dynasty over (northern) Israel. However, the Lord surely knew that Saul would not measure up to the challenge set before him. God had chosen Saul because he wanted him to serve as a negative example in contrast to David, whose behavior was so different. This, then, set the stage for the introduction of the legitimate kingship as God had always intended it.

· C H A P T E R   3 5 ·

An Evil Spirit
from the Lord
Tormented Saul

*So Samuel took the horn of oil and anointed [David]
in the presence of his brothers, and from that day on
the Spirit of the LORD came upon David in power.
Samuel then went to Ramah. Now the Spirit of the LORD
had departed from Saul, and an evil spirit
from the LORD tormented him.*
1 SAMUEL 16:13-14

Just as the prophet Samuel anointed David as the next king, King Saul became bereft of the Spirit of God and as a result fell into ugly bouts of melancholia, which were attributed to an evil spirit sent from the Lord. Therein lies our theological problem.

Is this similar to a theme in tales of the Greek gods and goddesses—whom the gods wish to destroy they first drive mad? Surely the depth of Saul's morose sadness cannot be attributed to a brief physical malady or a single bad day.

Saul's bouts of melancholy were attributed, instead, to the Lord, just as the lying spirit in Ahab's false prophets was.[1] The same phenomenon can be seen in Judges 9:23: "God sent an evil spirit between Abimelech and the citizens of Shechem."

The Spirit of God had overwhelmed Saul when he assumed the new role as king over the land (1 Sam 10:6, 10; 11:6). Exactly what the Spirit's presence with Saul entailed is not explained, but it probably included the gift of government, the gift of wisdom and prudence in civil matters and a spirit of fortitude and courage. These gifts can be extrapolated from the evidences that after Saul was anointed king, he immediately shed his previous shyness and reticence to be in the public eye.

But all of this was lost as suddenly as it had been gained. What explanation can we give for such a radical shift and reversion of his personality?

The ancient historian Josephus explained the "evil spirit from the Lord" as follows: "But as for Saul, some strange and demonical disorders came upon him, and brought upon him such suffocations as were ready to choke him" (Antiquities 6.8.2). Keil and Delitzsch, in their famous commentary on this passage, likewise attributed Saul's problem to demon possession. They specified that this "was not merely an inward feeling of depression at the rejection announced to him, . . . but a higher evil power, which took possession of him, and not only deprived him of his peace of mind, but stirred up the feelings, ideas, imagination, and thoughts of his soul to such an extent that at times it drove him even into madness. This demon is called 'an evil spirit [coming] from Jehovah' because Jehovah sent it as a punishment."[2]

A second suggestion is that this evil spirit was a messenger, by analogy with the situation in 1 Kings 22:20-23. This unspecified messenger did his work by the permission of God.

The third and final suggestion we can offer is that this evil spirit was a "spirit of discontent" created in Saul's heart by God because of his continued disobedience.

Whatever the malady was, and whatever its source, one of the temporary cures for its torments was music (v. 16). David's harp playing would soothe Saul's frenzied condition, so that he would once again gain control of his emotions and actions (1 Sam 16:14-23). In such times, "relief would come to Saul; he would feel better" (v. 23).

We conclude that all this happened by the permission of God rather than as a result of his directive will, for God cannot be the author of anything evil. But the exact source of Saul's torment cannot be determined with any degree of certitude. The Lord may well have used a messenger, or even just an annoying sense of disquietude and discontent. Yet if Saul really was a believer—and I think there are enough evidences to affirm that he was—then it is difficult to see how he could have been possessed by a demon. Whether believers can be possessed by demons, however, is still being debated by theologians.

Notes

[1] See Walter C. Kaiser, Jr., *Hard Sayings of the Old Testament* (Downers Grove, Ill.: InterVarsity Press, 1988), chap. 31.

[2] Johann Karl Friedrich Keil and Franz Delitzsch, *Biblical Commentary on the Books of Samuel* (Grand Rapids: Eerdmans, 1950), p. 170.

Whose Son Are You, Young Man?

Then Saul sent word to Jesse, saying, "Allow David to
remain in my service, for I am pleased with him."
1 SAMUEL 16:22

As Saul watched David going out to meet the Philistine,
he said to Abner, commander of the army, "Abner, whose son is that
young man?" Abner replied, "As surely as you live, O king, I don't know."
The king said, "Find out whose son this young man is." As soon as
David returned from killing the Philistine, Abner took him and brought
him before Saul, with David still holding the Philistine's head.
"Whose son are you, young man?" Saul asked.
1 SAMUEL 17:55-58

Saul's questions about the identity of David in 1 Samuel 17 create a rather difficult problem in light of 1 Samuel 16, especially verses 14-23. It would appear from chapter 16 that by the time of David's slaying of Goliath Saul had already been introduced to David and knew him quite well.

The traditional way of resolving this dilemma in nonevangel-

ical circles is to suppose that these two accounts stem from independent traditions. Thus the confusion over whether David's
debut at court preceded his conquest of the Philistine is unnec-
essary, since the stories come from different sources and do not
intend to reflect what really happened so much as teach a truth.
However, this resolution of the matter is not attractive to most
who take the claims of the Bible more straightforwardly.

Therefore, the point of the difficulty continues: how could
Saul—and Abner too—be ignorant about this lad who had been
Saul's armor-bearer and musician?

Some have blamed Saul's diseased and failing mental state. On
this view, the evil spirit from God had brought on a type of
mental malady that affected his memory. Persons suffering from
certain types of mania or insanity often forget the closest of their
friends.

Others have argued that the hustle and bustle of court life,
with its multiplicity of servants and attendants, meant that Saul
could have easily forgotten David, especially if the time was long
between David's service through music and his slaying of Goliath. Yet a long period of time does not appear to have separated
these events. Furthermore, David was a regular member of
Saul's retinue (1 Sam 16:21).

A third option tries to focus on the fact that Saul was not
asking for David's identity, which he knew well enough. Instead,
he was attempting to learn what his father's social position and
worth were, for he was concerned what type of stock his future
son-in-law might come from. (Remember, whoever was successful in killing Goliath would win the hand of Saul's daughter,
according to the terms of Saul's challenge.) While this might
explain Saul's motives, does it explain Abner's lack of knowledge?
Or must we posit that he also knew who David was, but had no
idea what his social status and lineage were? Possibly!

The most plausible explanation, and the one favored by most

older commentators, is that the four events in the history of Saul and David in 1 Samuel 16—18 are not given in chronological order. Instead, they are transposed, by a figure of speech known as *hysterologia*, in which something is put last that according to the usual order should be put first. For example, Genesis 10's account of the dispersion of the nations comes before the cause of it—the confusion of languages at the Tower of Babel in Genesis 11.

The fact that the order has been rearranged for special purposes in 1 Samuel 16—18 can be seen from the fact that the Vaticanus Manuscript of the Septuagint deletes twenty-nine verses in all (1 Sam 17:12-31 and 17:55—18:5).

E. W. Bullinger suggested that the text was rearranged in order to bring together certain facts, especially those about the Spirit of God. Thus in 1 Samuel 16:1-13 David is anointed and the Spirit of God comes upon him. Then, in order to contrast this impartation of the Spirit of God with the removal of the Spirit from Saul, 1 Samuel 16:14-23 is brought forward from later history. In the straightforward order of events, Bullinger suggests, it should follow 18:9.[1]

First Samuel 17:1—18:9 records an event earlier in the life of David, which is introduced here in a parenthetical way as an illustration of 1 Samuel 14:52. This section is just an instance of what 14:52 claims.

The whole section, therefore, has this construction:

A	16:1-13	David anointed. The Spirit comes on him.
B	16:14-23	Saul rejected. The Spirit departs from him. An evil spirit torments him.
A	17:1—18:9	David. An earlier incident in his life.
B	18:10-30	Saul. The Spirit departs and an evil spirit troubles him.

Thus, the narration alternates between David and Saul, creating a didactic contrast between the Spirit of God and the evil spirit that tormented Saul. The focus is on the spiritual state of the two men, not the historical order of events.

All too frequently, the books of Joshua, Judges, Samuel and Kings are given the label "Historical Books" rather than the more correct label "Earlier Prophets." They aim at teaching lessons from the prophetic eye of inspiration rather than simply providing a chronicle of how events occurred in time and history.

That these texts appear in topical, rather than chronological, order is the best explanation, especially when we note how the theology of the text is embedded in it.

Note

[1]E. W. Bullinger, *Figures of Speech* (1898; reprint ed., Grand Rapids: Baker, 1968), pp. 706-7.

Saul Stripped Off His Robes and Prophesied

*Word came to Saul: "David is in Naioth at Ramah"; so he sent men
to capture him. But when they saw a group of prophets prophesying,
with Samuel standing there as their leader, the Spirit of God
came upon Saul's men and they also prophesied. Saul was told about it,
and he sent more men, and they prophesied too. Saul sent men a third time,
and they also prophesied. Finally, he himself left for Ramah and went
to the great cistern at Secu. And he asked, "Where are Samuel and David?"
"Over in Naioth at Ramah," they said.
So Saul went to Naioth at Ramah. But the Spirit of God came even
upon him, and he walked along prophesying until he came to Naioth.
He stripped off his robes and also prophesied in Samuel's presence.
He lay that way all that day and night. This is why people say,
"Is Saul also among the prophets?"*
1 SAMUEL 19:19-24

Seeking a naturalistic explanation for the phenomenon of prophecy in
the Old Testament, some have theorized that such powers derived from ecstatic experiences in which the prophet wandered
outside his own consciousness during a period of artistic creation. One of the passages used to sustain such a thesis is 1 Samuel 19:19-24.

Quite apart from the issue of ecstasy in prophecy are two other matters. Could a king also be a prophet? And did the king really strip off all his clothes as a result of this powerful experience of prophesying? Surely this is one of the most curious texts in the Old Testament.

The story told here is clear enough. In a jealous rage over David's popularity and success, Saul was bent on capturing David. No doubt rumors were now spreading that Samuel had anointed David as king in place of the then-reigning Saul.

Saul sent three different groups of messengers to apprehend David, who had fled from Saul to join Samuel at his prophetic school at Ramah. All three groups encountered Samuel's band of prophets prophesying. And each of the groups of messengers began to prophesy as well.

At last, Saul had had enough and decided to go in search of David himself. While he was still on the way, however, the "Spirit of God" came on him, so that he too prophesied. Later, after coming to where the others were, he removed some of his clothing and lay in an apparent stupor the rest of that day and the following night.

Each of the three problems raised by this text deserves some response based on the meaning of certain words used in this context and other similar contexts.

It has been claimed that the Greeks thought artistic genius was always accompanied by a degree of madness; thus, those who prophesied must have similarly experienced "ecstasy"—a word literally meaning "to stand apart from or outside oneself." Furthermore, it was argued that the behavior of the Canaanite prophets of Baal on Mount Carmel was just like that of earlier Israelite prophets.

But the verb *to prophesy*, as used in this context, does not mean "to act violently" or "to be mad." The Old Testament makes a clear distinction between the prophets of Canaan and those under the inspiration of God.

Only three Old Testament passages have been used as evidence that "to prophesy" entails a temporary madness and standing apart from oneself. These three passages, however, record the estimates of others rather than God's estimates of prophets and the source of their inspiration. In 2 Kings 9:11, a young prophet sent by Elisha to anoint Jehu as king is called a "madman" *(meshugga')* by the soldiers who are sitting in Jehu's barracks. Their label is hardly a statement from God or a source of normative teaching. The Bible simply records that that is what these men thought of prophets—an attitude not altogether dissimilar from that held today by some about the clergy. A second text, Jeremiah 29:26, quotes a certain Shemaiah, then captive in Babylon, from a letter where he too opines: "Every man that is mad *[meshugga']* makes himself a prophet" (my translation). In the final text, Hosea 9:7, Hosea characterizes a point in Israel's thinking by saying, "The prophet is considered a fool, the inspired man a maniac *[meshugga']*."

None of these three texts demonstrates that the verb *to prophesy* legitimately carries the connotation of madness. Instead, they simply show that many associated prophecy with madness in an attempt to stigmatize the work of real prophets. It was the ancient equivalent of the Elmer Gantry image of Christian ministers today!

As for Saul's being "naked" all day and night, the term used might just as well refer to his being partially disrobed. It seems to be used with the latter meaning in Job 22:6; 24:7; Isaiah 58:7; and probably Isaiah 20:2-3, where Isaiah is said to have walked "stripped and barefoot for three years." Saul probably stripped off his outer garment, leaving only the long tunic beneath.

The figure of speech involved here is synecdoche, in which the whole stands for a part. Thus, *naked* or *stripped* is used to mean "scantily clad" or "poorly clothed." Beside the passages already mentioned, we should add Matthew 25:36, 43; John 21:7; James 2:15; and 1 Corinthians 4:11 as examples of the same usage.

In an attempt to shore up the failing theory of ecstasy, some have pointed to verse 24 as evidence that Saul was "beside himself"—again, the etymology of our word *ecstasy*. However, this will not work since the verb in verse 24 simply means "to put off" a garment (by opening it and unfolding it; the verb's other meaning is "to expand, to spread out, to extend"). There is no evidence that it means "to stand beside oneself" or anything like that.

What about the apparent stupor? Did Saul momentarily lose his sanity? While the three groups of messengers experienced a strong influence of the Spirit of God, it was Saul, we may rightfully conclude, who fell under the strongest work of the Spirit.

The Spirit fell more powerfully on Saul than on the messengers because Saul had more stubbornly resisted the will of God. In this manner, God graciously warned Saul that he was kicking against the very will of God, not just against a shepherd-boy rival. The overmastering influence that came on Saul was to convince him that his struggle was with God and not with David. His action in sending the three groups to capture David had been in defiance of God himself, so he had to be graphically warned. As a result, the king also, but unexpectedly, prophesied. So surprised were all around them that a proverb subsequently arose to characterize events that ran against ordinary expectations: "Is Saul also among the prophets?" (v. 24). Kings normally did not expect to receive the gift of prophecy. But here God did the extraordinary in order to move a recalcitrant king's heart to see the error of his ways.

The noun *prophecy* and verb *to prophesy* appear more than three hundred times in the Old Testament. Often outbursts of exuberant praise or of deep grief were connected with prophesying. But there seems to be no evidence for ecstasy as envisioned by some who treat these texts—that is, a wild, uncontrollable enthusiasm that forced the individual to go temporarily mad or insane. And if we dilute the meaning of *ecstasy* so as to take away the negative implications—like those attached to the Greek's theory that artists only drew, composed or wrote when temporarily overcome with madness—the term becomes so bland that it loses its significance. In that case we all might qualify to join the band of the prophets. Certainly, nothing in this text suggests the dancing, raving and loss of consciousness sometimes seen in contemporary extrabiblical phenomena.

· C H A P T E R 3 8 ·

Saul
and the Witch
of Endor

Saul then said to his attendants, "Find me a woman who is a medium,
so I may go and inquire of her." . . .
So Saul disguised himself, putting on other clothes, and at night
he and two men went to the woman. "Consult a spirit for me,"
he said, "and bring up for me the one I name." . . .
Then Saul knew it was Samuel. . . . Samuel said to Saul, "Why have you
disturbed me by bringing me up? . . . Why do you consult me, now that
the LORD has turned away from you and become your enemy?"

1 SAMUEL 28:7-8, 14-16

The problems raised by the account of Saul's encounter with the witch of Endor in 1 Samuel 28 are legion! To begin with, spiritism, witches, mediums and necromancers (those who communicate with the dead) are not approved in Scripture. In fact, a number of stern passages warn against any involvement with or practice of these satanic arts. For example, Deuteronomy 18:9-12 includes these practices in a list of nine abominations that stand in opposition to revelation from God through his prophets. Exodus

22:18 denies sorceresses the right to live. Leviticus 19:26, 31; and 20:6, 27 likewise sternly caution against practicing or consulting a medium, a sorceress or anyone who practices divination. God would set his face against that person. Those cultivating these arts were to be put to death—the community was not to tolerate them, for what they did was so heinous that it was the very antithesis of the revelation that came from God (see Jer 27:9-10).

But there are other issues as well. Did the witch of Endor really have supernatural powers from Satan, which enabled her to bring Samuel up from the dead? Or was Samuel's appearance not literal, merely the product of psychological impressions? Perhaps it was a demon or Satan himself that impersonated Samuel. Or perhaps the whole thing was a trick played on Saul. Which is the correct view? And how does such a view fit in with the rest of biblical revelation?

The most prevalent view among orthodox commentators is that there was a genuine appearance of Samuel brought about by God himself. The main piece of evidence favoring this interpretation is 1 Chronicles 10:13-14: "Saul died because he was unfaithful to the LORD; he did not keep the word of the LORD and even consulted a medium for guidance, and did not inquire of the LORD." The Septuagint reading of this text adds: "Saul asked counsel of her that had a familiar spirit to inquire of her, and Samuel made answer to him." Moreover, the medium must not have been accustomed to having her necromancies work, for when she saw Samuel, she cried out in a scream that let Saul know that something new and different was happening, even for a hardened practitioner of this trade. This night her so-called arts were working beyond her usual expectations.

Then, too, the fact that Saul bowed in obeisance indicates that this probably was a real appearance of Samuel. What seems to have convinced Saul was the witch's description of Samuel's appearance. She reported that Samuel was wearing the characteristic "robe" *(me'il)*. That was the very robe Saul had seized and ripped as Samuel declared that the kingdom had been ripped out of his hand (1 Sam 15:27-28).

Is Samuel's statement to Saul in verse 15 proof that the witch had brought Samuel back from the dead? The message delivered by this shade or apparition sounds as if it could well have been from Samuel and from God. Therefore, it is entirely possible that this was a real apparition of Samuel. As to whether Samuel appeared physically, in a body, we conclude that the text does not suggest that he did, nor does Christian theology accord with such a view. But there can be little doubt that there was an appearance of Samuel's spirit or ghost. The witch herself, in her startled condition, claimed that what she saw was a "god" *('elohim,* v. 13) coming up out of the earth. The most probable interpretation of this term *'elohim* is the "spirit" of a deceased person. This implies an authentic appearance of the dead, but one that did not result from her witchcraft. Instead, it was God's final means of bringing a word to a king who insisted on going his own way.

Those who have argued for a psychological impression face two objections. The first is the woman's shriek of horror in verse 12. She would not have screamed if the spirit had been merely Saul's hallucination, produced by psychological excitement. The second objection is that not only does the text imply that the woman talked with Samuel but so did Saul. Even more convincing is the fact that what Samuel is purported to have said turned out to be true!

As for the demon impersonation theory, some of the same objections apply. The text represents this as a real happening, not an impersonation. Of course Satan does appear as "an angel of light" (2 Cor 11:14), but there is reason to suppose that this is what is going on here.

Our conclusion is that God allowed Samuel's spirit to appear to give Saul one more warning about the evil of his ways.

One of the reasons believers are warned to stay away from spiritists, mediums and necromancers is that some do have powers supplied to them from the netherworld. Whether the witch accomplished her feat by the power of Satan or under the mighty hand of God we may never know in this life. Of course, all that happens must be allowed or directed by God. Thus the question is finally whether it was his directive or permissive will that brought up Samuel. If it were the later, did the witch apply for satanic powers, or was she a total fraud who was taught a lesson about the overwhelming power of God through this experience? In the final analysis, we are unable to make a firm choice between these two possibilities.

The Death
of David and
Bathsheba's Son

[David's] servants asked him, "Why are you acting this way?
While the child was alive, you fasted and wept, but now that the child
is dead, you get up and eat!"
He answered, "While the child was still alive, I fasted and wept.
I thought, 'Who knows? The LORD may be gracious to me and let the child live.'
But now that he is dead, why should I fast? Can I bring him back again?
I will go to him, but he will not return to me."
2 SAMUEL 12:21-23

What are the prospects of the dead in the Old Testament? And what
shall we say about those who die in infancy and thus have never
heard about the wonderful grace of our Lord? Is their future
gloomy and dark, without hope? These are some of the questions
raised by this passage on the child born to David and Bathsheba
as a result of their adulterous act.

Several passages in the Old Testament show that death is not
the absolute end of all life. For example, 1 Samuel 28:15-19 says
that upon the death of Saul and his sons in battle the next day,

they would join Samuel, who was already dead, yet here was conscious and able to speak.

Likewise, David affirmed his confidence that he would one day go to meet his deceased son; in the meantime, it was impossible for his son to come and join him back on earth. Surely this implies that the son consciously and actually existed at the time of David's speaking, even though it was impossible for the son to transcend the boundaries set by death.

If David's expectation was to see God and to be with God after death, he believed that his son would also be in the presence of God, even though that son never had the opportunity to hear about the gospel or to respond to its offer of grace. Apparently, the grace of God has made provisions that go beyond those that apply to all who can hear or read about God's revelation of his grace in his Word and in his Son, Jesus.

Those psalms of David in which the dead are said to lack any knowledge or remembrance of God are highly poetical and figurative expressions of how unnatural and violent death is. Death will continue to separate the living from each other and from the use of their bodies until Christ returns to restore what has been lost. Psalm 6:5 expresses the psalmist's hatred of death, saying that after we have died people tend to forget us: "No one remembers you when he is dead." "You" refers to the dead person, not to God as the King James Version suggests: "For in death there is no remembrance of thee." Isn't it better, David continues, for people to be alive so that they can praise God? "Who praises you from the grave?" The dead are without the ability to lift praises to God. That seems to be David's burden.

Neither can Ecclesiastes 9:5-6 count against the position we have taken here. To claim that "the dead know nothing" is not to deny any hope beyond the grave. The point of Ecclesiastes is limited to what can be observed from a strictly human point of view, "under the sun." Its statement that the dead "have no further reward" (9:5) is reminiscent of Jesus' words, "As long as it is day [while we are still alive], we must do the work of him who sent me. Night is coming, when no one can work" (Jn 9:4).

In 2 Samuel 12:23 David does not take the perspective of this life—as some of these other passages do—but the perspective of an eternity with God. And from that perspective, there is much to hope for.

While it is true that the Lord allowed David's child to die, it is not true that God thereby gave tacit approval to infanticide. The killing of babies is sternly forbidden in Scripture as an abomination to God (Lev 18:21; Deut 12:31; 2 Chron 28:3; Is 57:5; Jer 19:4-7). Even when infanticide was practiced in the name of religion, as it was in the worship of Molech, it earned the wrath of God.

David took comfort in the hope that God would take this little one to himself. He left the child, therefore, to the grace of God, expressing his hope of rejoining that child in the future. There *is* life after death, even for infants who die before they have seen any, or many, days.

David
and His
Concubines

When David returned to his palace in Jerusalem,
he took the ten concubines he had left to take care of the palace
and put them in a house under guard. He provided for them,
but did not lie with them. They were kept in confinement
till the day of their death, living as widows.
2 SAMUEL 20:3

T *he institution of concubinage seems to many of us as wrong and as* evil as the institution of slavery. And so it was from an Old Testament point of view as well.

Genesis 2:21-24 presents us with God's normative instructions for marriage: one man was to be joined to one woman so as to become one flesh.

Polygamy appears for the first time in Genesis 4:19, when Lamech became the first bigamist in marrying two wives, Adah and Zillah. No other recorded instances of polygamy exist from Shem to Terah, the father of Abraham (except for the episode in Gen 6:1-7).

Was polygamy (with its correlative concubinage) ever a lawful practice in the Old Testament? No permission can be recited from the text for any such institution or practice. To support it, one could appeal only to illustrations in the lives of a rather select number of persons. None of these examples has the force of normative theology. The Bible merely describes what some did; it never condones their polygamy, nor does it make their practices normative for that time or later times.

From the beginning of time up to 931 B.C., when the kingdom was divided after Solomon's day, there are only fifteen examples of polygamy in the Old Testament: Lamech, the "sons of God" in Genesis 6:1-7, Abraham's brother Nahor, Abraham, Esau, Jacob, Gideon, Jair, Ibzan, Abdon, Samson, Elkanah, Saul, David and Solomon. In the divided monarchy, Rehoboam, Abijah, Ahab and Jehoram all were bigamists, and possibly Joash (depending on how we interpret "for him" or "for himself" in 2 Chron 24:2-3). This gives us a total of nineteen instances, and among them thirteen were persons of absolute power whom no one could call into judgment except God.

The despotic way in which the rulers of Genesis 6:1-7 took as many wives as they pleased is censured by Scripture, as are those who indulged in adulterous and polygamous behavior prior to the flood. The Law of Moses also censures those who violate God's prescription of monogamous marriage. Scripture does not, however, always pause to state the obvious or to moralize on the events that it records.

Those who say the Old Testament gave direct or implied permission for polygamy usually point to four passages: Exodus 21:7-11, Leviticus 18:18, Deuteronomy 21:15-17 and 2 Samuel 12:7-8. Each of these texts has had a history of incorrect interpretation.[1]

There is no suggestion of a second marriage with "marital rights" in Exodus 21:10, for the word translated "marital rights" should be rendered "oil" or "ointments." The text says that a man who has purchased a female servant (perhaps to fulfill a debt) must continue to provide for her if he proposes marriage and then decides not to consummate it. Leviticus 18:18 does not imply that a man may marry a second wife so long as she is not a sister to the one he already has. Instead, it prohibits his marrying his wife's sister during the lifetime of his wife, since having her sister as a rival would vex her. Likewise, Deuteronomy 21:15-17 legislates the rights of the firstborn, regardless of whether that child is the son of the preferred wife or of the wife who is not loved. To contend, as some do, that legislation on rights within polygamy tacitly condones polygamy makes about as much sense as saying that Deuteronomy 18:18 approves of harlotry since it prohibits bringing the wages earned by harlotry into the house of the Lord for any vow.

Finally, 2 Samuel 12:7-8 supplies no encouragement to polygamy when it says that all that Saul had, including his wives, were to be David's possessions. Nowhere in all the lists of David's wives are Saul's two wives listed; hence the expression must be a stereotypic formula signifying that everything in principle was turned over for David's disposition.

Everywhere in the Old Testament the normative teaching on marriage remains the same. One's wife, according to Psalm 128:3, was to be a fruitful vine. Only one would be blessed by God.

The best statement on monogamous marriage is found in the little allegory of Proverbs 5:15-21. The husband is to be devoted to the wife of his youth and to "drink water from [his] own cistern." Her breasts alone are to satisfy him always (v. 19). Why would he ever be captivated by the love of another?

Malachi 2:14 says that God is a witness to all weddings and contends for the "wife of [our] youth," who is all too frequently left at the altar in tears because of the violence caused by divorce

(or any of marriage's other perversions). Jeremiah had to rebuke
the men of his own generation who were "neighing for another
man's wife" (Jer 5:8). Had polygamy been customarily or even
tacitly approved, this text of Jeremiah would have had to record
"another man's *wives*." Furthermore, these men's sin would have
had a ready solution: they should look around and acquire several
new wives on their own, instead of seeking those who were
already taken! No, polygamy never was God's order for marriage
in the Old Testament. David sinned, therefore, in having a plu-
rality of wives. But what of his putting the ten concubines under
guard after his son Absalom his son had violated them in a palace
coup?

The answer this time is one of political expediency of that day.
If David had had relations with any one of them and she conceived, it would be difficult to know whether the son was his or
Absalom's. And he dare not turn these women out in the streets,
for that would have violated the rules of compassion and could
have produced another contender to the throne, since all who
had any contact with the king, even as a concubine, could lay
some claim to the throne in the future.

Thus, David took the only course he could under such circumstances. There is no doubt about it: he had sown to the wind and
now he must reap the whirlwind. God had never changed his
mind about the appropriateness of one wife for one husband to
become one flesh.

Note

[1]For more details, see Walter C. Kaiser, Jr., *Toward Old Testament Ethics* (Grand
Rapids: Zondervan, 1983), pp. 184-90.

·CHAPTER 41·

Avenging the Violation of Joshua's Oath

During the reign of David, there was a famine for three successive years;
so David sought the face of the LORD. The LORD said, "It is on account of Saul
and his blood-stained house; it is because he put the Gibeonites to death."
The king summoned the Gibeonites. . . .
They answered the king, "As for the man who destroyed us and plotted
against us so that we have been decimated and have no place anywhere
in Israel, let seven of his male descendants be given to us to be killed and
exposed before the Lord at Gibeah of Saul—the Lord's chosen one."
So the king said, "I will give them to you."
2 SAMUEL 21:1-2, 5-6

Few stories in the Old Testament are more difficult for individualistic Westerners to understand than this one told in 2 Samuel 21.

The background for this episode goes all the way back to the days of Joshua. Under the pretense of being from afar, the pre-Israelite inhabitants of Canaan, known variously as Hivites (Josh 9:7) and Amorites (2 Sam 21:2), precipitously won a treaty from Joshua and the elders, who later discovered that these people were not from a great distance, but in fact lived right in the path of the ongoing conquest. Reluctantly, but surely, Joshua and the elders conceded that they had sworn an oath before Yahweh that they would do these people no harm. So the Gibeonites remained untouched in Israel, though they were required to serve as hewers of wood and drawers of water for the house of God (see Josh 9 for details).

Psalm 15:4 makes it a point of honor to keep one's oath, even when it hurts. Unfortunately, in his touted zeal for Israel Saul had violated Joshua's ancient oath and brought "blood-guiltiness" on the whole land. Apparently, some dissatisfaction with the Gibeonites had provided Saul with a pretext to vent his prejudices against these non-Jews who lived in the midst of the Israelites. And the Lord, who inspects all that is said and done on earth, required justice to be done. Thus it was that even as late as David's reign a plague fell on all the land for three successive years. Having asked the Lord why they were experiencing this continual drought, David was told of the injustice that had been done to the Gibeonites. Whether David had known about this wrongdoing previously is not discussed in the text.

When David consulted with the Gibeonites, asking what they wished by way of compensation for Saul's attack on them, they demanded seven of Saul's sons to be killed and displayed in Saul's home and capital city, Gibeah. David agreed to their request.

Therein lies our problem. What made David agree to such a hideous retribution, and how could that compensate the Gibeonites? And why did it satisfy divine justice (since the rains came after the act had been completed)? Does God favor human sacrifice? Each of these questions deserves an answer.

The Mosaic Law clearly prohibits human sacrifice and speaks scornfully of those who ordered their sons to be offered to the false god Molech (Lev 18:21; 20:2). But our text does not depict the killing of Saul's descendants as an offering to anyone, so this is not a case of sacrifice.

Neither does the Old Testament deny the principle of individualism, so dear to (and so abused by) Westerners. Deuteronomy 24:16 teaches that "fathers shall not be put to death for their children, nor children put to death for their fathers; each is to die for his own sin." Yet sometimes factors beyond individual responsibility are at work in a world of sin.

The Old Testament also reminds us of our corporate involvement, through which a member of a group can be held fully responsible for an action of the group, even though he or she personally may have had nothing to do with that act. Thus the whole group may be treated as a unit or through a representative. This is not to argue for a type of collectivism or a rejection of individual responsibility. Ten righteous men could have preserved Sodom and Gomorrah (Gen 18). A righteous man blesses his children after him (Prov 11:21). On the flip side, however, the sin of few can bring judgment on the many, as in the story of the Korah, Dathan and Abiram incident in Numbers 16.

Certainly, there was to be collective punishment in Israel when a whole city was drawn into idolatrous worship at the incitement of a few good-for-nothing fellows (Deut 13:12-16). Complicity in the crime perpetrated against Naboth, in the taking of his land and life by the throne, led to judgment against the royal house, since there was no repentance in the interim (1 Kings 21; 2 Kings 10:1-11).

David granted the Gibeonites' request because, according to the Law of Moses, "bloodshed pollutes the land, and atonement cannot be made for the land on which blood has been shed, except by the blood of the one who shed it" (Num 35:33). This being so, the members of Saul's house had to be delivered over to the Gibeonites. Hope of the land's deliverance from the judgment of God did not lie in any other avenue. In fact, 2 Samuel 21:3 specifically mentions "making expiation" or "atonement" *(kapar)*. (The NIV translates it as "make amends"!) The Gibeonites insisted that it was not possible for them to accept a substitute such as "silver or gold" in this case (v. 4). The seriousness of the crime demanded something more, as Numbers 35:31, 33 teaches.

David was careful to spare Mephibosheth, the recently discovered son of Jonathan, with whom David had made a covenant prior to Jonathan's death (1 Sam 18:3; 20:8, 16). But he delivered to the Gibeonites two sons of Rizpah, a concubine of Saul, and five sons of Saul's eldest daughter, Merab.

After killing them, the Gibeonites impaled the bodies on stakes and left them hanging in Saul's home town of Gibeah as a rebuke to all who would attempt genocide, as Saul apparently had. According to Deuteronomy 21:22-23, persons who were executed were not to remain hanging through the night upon a stake, but were to be buried before evening. This law, however, did not appear to have any application to this case, where expiation of guilt for the whole land was concerned, and where non-Israelite Gibeonites were involved. It seems that the bodies remained on display until the famine actually ended; they were taken down as the rains began to fall.

Though David complied with the Gibeonite request, there is nothing in the text that suggests that he engineered the situation so as to get rid of any potential rivals from Saul's line. Rather, the text stresses how important it is to honor covenants made before God. In the so-called second plague prayer given by the Hittite king Mursilis II (fourteenth century B.C.), he similarly blames a twenty-year famine in his land on a previous ruler's breach of a treaty between the Hittites and the Egyptians. How much more accountable would Israel be for a similar violation before Yahweh!

One traitor can affect the outcome of a whole battle and the lives of a whole army. So, too, the acts of those who rule on behalf of a whole nation can affect all either for good or for ill.

Blood-guiltiness left on the land, whether through the betrayal of a covenant made before God or through a failure to put to death those who deliberately took the lives of innocent victims, must be avenged on those who caused the guilt. Otherwise, the land will languish under the hand of God's judgment.

Making Clear the Book of the Law

They read from the Book of the Law of God,
making it clear and giving the meaning so that the people
could understand what was being read.
NEHEMIAH 8:8

T he issue in this verse is rather simple, but far-reaching in its effects. It concerns the word here translated as "making it clear" *(meparash)*. Much has been written on this term, since some prefer to render it "to translate." This would mean that the exiles who had returned from seventy years of captivity in Babylon had become fluent in Aramaic, but had lost their ability to understand the text of the Law as it was read it Hebrew.

But if these Jews really had lost their knowledge of Hebrew, then we must wonder why it is that such postexilic books as 1 and 2 Chronicles, Ezra, Nehemiah, Esther, Haggai, Zechariah and Malachi were written in Hebrew. If the writers of these texts wanted to reach the Jewish audience of the fifth and fourth centuries

B.C., why did they choose to use an archaic language that the people no longer grasped? Something does not seem to fit.

Approximately one week after the returnees had completed the walls of Jerusalem (Neh 6:15; 7:1), the people assembled in the square in front of the famous Water Gate (Neh 3:26). There Ezra, the scribe, began a public reading of the Torah of Moses (Neh 8:1).

Although Ezra is not recorded as having had a major part in the fifty-two-day rebuilding of the walls of Jerusalem, he now appeared on the scene as a spiritual leader and as the reader of the Law of God. Ezra had led an earlier return of some fifty thousand Jews from Babylon in 458 B.C. Nehemiah had come later, in 445 B.C., as a civil leader leading an aroused populace to quickly rebuild the walls of the holy city.

The people were assembled in front of the Water Gate, which is on the east wall of the city of Jerusalem. This gate led to the famous Gihon Spring, the main source of water for Jerusalem.

It was the first day of the month of Tishri, the day designated as the Feast of Trumpets (Num 29:1; Lev 23:24). As specified by the Law, this was a day of rest and worship. It was a time of preparation for the most significant day in Israel's religious calendar, the Day of Atonement, celebrated on the tenth of Tishri (approximately our September/October).

The assembly included all men, women, and children who could understand (Neh 8:2). The meeting began early in the morning, at the break of day (v. 3), and Ezra read until midday— approximately six hours! He spoke from a wooden platform that accommodated not only his pulpit but also the thirteen Levites who helped him in this work. Just how these thirteen men functioned is not altogether clear. Did they assist him in the reading of the Law, or did they split the people up into small groups from time to time to assist them in their comprehension of what was being read?

As the Book of the Law was opened, the people stood to show their respect for the Word of God. Prior to the reading, however, Ezra led the people in a prayer of praise to the Lord their God. The people responded with "Amen! Amen!" as they lifted their hands and bowed down in worship to the Lord (v. 6).

It is at this point that our problematic verse appears. What does *meparash* mean? Does it mean to "translate"—in this case, from Hebrew into the cognate tongue of Aramaic—or does it mean to give an exposition of the passage and make the sense clear?

The root from which this word in verse 8 comes, *parash*, has the basic meaning "to make distinct, or separate." It could refer to the way the words were distinctly articulated, or better still, the Law's being read and expounded section by section. The word *parasha*, a cognate of our term, was used by the Hebrew Massoretic scribes to speak of dividing the Pentateuch into paragraphs or sections for each reading. Therefore, we cannot agree that the Levites were mere translators for the people. They "broke out" the standard Pentateuchal sections and followed the readings with exposition, "giving the meaning so the people could understand what was being read" (v. 8b).

The motive for observing this Feast of Trumpets (or Rosh Hashanah, the Jewish New Year's Day) was the people's thanksgiving for God's gracious assistance in rebuilding the wall. This goodness of God led them instinctively to want to hear more of God's Word. They stood by the hour to listen intently to that Word and to have it explained to them.

There is no need to wonder why so many postexilic books of the Old Testament were written in Hebrew. The only alleged evidence that the Jewish returnees could not speak Hebrew is this one word in Nehemiah 8:8, and there are no linguistic grounds for thinking that it means "translating."

· C H A P T E R 4 3 ·

Esther for
Such a Time
as This

*[Mordecai said], "Do not think that because you are in the king's
house you alone of all the Jews will escape. For if you remain silent
at this time, relief and deliverance for the Jews will arise from
another place, but you and your father's family will perish.
And who knows but that you have come to royal position
for such a time as this?"*
ESTHER 4:13-14

Why does the book of Esther, which so wonderfully illustrates the
doctrine of the providence of God, never once use the name of
God? And what does this strange saying in verse 14 mean? The
sentence contains a figure of speech known as *aposiopesis*—a sudden breaking off of what was being said or written, so that the
mind is more impressed by what is left unsaid, it being too wonderful, solemn or awful to verbalize. In English this figure is
sometimes called the "sudden silence."

Taking the last problem first, it must be noted that the last
clause in verse 14 is usually understood to mean: "And who

knows whether you have not for a time like this attained royalty?" This makes very good sense, but it cannot be justified linguistically. The sentence contains an *aposiopesis* or sudden silence, since the object of "who knows" is unexpressed. It is incorrect to translate the verse with a conditional "whether . . . not" (as in the RSV, for example) rather than "but that." The omitted clause in the *aposiopesis* would be "what might not have been done." The resulting translation, with the suppressed clause now included, would be: "Who knows *what might not have been done* but that you attained to royalty for such a time as this?"

"Who knows" can also be translated "perhaps." On that rendering, Mordecai would have said, "Perhaps you have attained to royalty [to the dignity of being queen] for a time like this [to use your position to deliver your people]." Thus Mordecai's speech contains an urgent appeal to Esther to use her high position in order to preserve her fellow Jews from destruction.

The absence of God's name from the book must also be faced. Many interpreters rightly focus on the phrase "another place" in verse 14 ("if you remain silent at this time, relief and deliverance for the Jews will arise from another place"). This particular phrase is one of the most debated yet also most crucial in the book of Esther.

Did Mordecai have another individual in mind? Or did he think that some other world power would arise to deliver the Jews out of this empire?

Surely the Greek "A" text, Josephus, and 1 and 2 Targums are correct in seeing in "another place" a veiled reference to God, just as the New Testament uses "kingdom of heaven" as a circumlocution for "the Kingdom of God" and as 1 Maccabees 16:3 uses "mercy" as a veiled allusion to God. Often in later Talmudic literature, the word "place" (*maqom*) would be used in place of the name of God.

Furthermore, the fact that Esther asked the community of

Jews to fast on her behalf (Esther 4:16) indicates that she and they sought divine help. Moreover, faith in the providence of God and his hand in history is illustrated throughout the book. In Esther, the wonderful works of God declare his name; there is no need to spell out that name when his hand and presence can be detected everywhere.

Does Job Fear God for Nothing?

One day the angels came to present themselves before the LORD,
and Satan also came with them. . . .
Then the LORD said to Satan, "Have you considered my servant Job?
There is no one on earth like him; he is blameless and upright,
a man who fears God and shuns evil."
"Does Job fear God for nothing?" Satan replied. "Have you not put
a hedge around him and his household and everything he has?
You have blessed the work of his hands, so that his flocks and his herds
are spread throughout the land. But stretch out your hand and strike
everything he has, and he will surely curse you to your face."
The LORD said to Satan, "Very well, then, everything he has is in your hands,
but on the man himself do not lay a finger."
JOB 1:6-12

Several points arrest our attention as we read this well-known story about the trials of that old patriarch Job. First of all, who are these angels ("sons of God") who come to present themselves before God in verse 6? And who is "Satan"? Can he be the being that the New Testament calls by the same name? If he is, what on earth is he doing appearing before God? Finally, why does

God permit Job to be tested, since the New Testament book of James makes it clear that God tempts no one?

This passage gives us a glimpse of a most extraordinary scene in the invisible world. Its most surprising feature is the presence of Satan, whom we otherwise know as the Prince of Darkness. This seems such an astonishing and unusual event that we are led to think that the Satan of the book of Job cannot be the Satan of later Scriptures. How could he have anything to do with light and the presence of God?

A moment's reflection, however, will show that there is no dichotomy between the Satan of the Old Testament and the Satan of the New Testament. There is profound meaning in representing Satan as appearing before God, for he is thereby designated as subordinate and in subjection to divine control. He cannot act on his own discretion or without any boundaries. He must receive permission from the Sovereign Lord.

It used to be fashionable in scholarship to regard Satan in the book of Job as a creation of the author's fancy, due to the paucity of references to Satan in the Old Testament. Others attributed the origin of a concept of a personage of evil to Persia, perhaps the character Ahriman. But there are no striking similarities between Satan and Ahriman, nor bases for conjecturing a link between them.

No, Satan is not the phantom of some author's imagination or an import from an ancient Near Eastern culture. Neither is he an impartial executor of judgment and overseer of morality, for he denies everything that God affirms. He has no love toward God and is bent on destroying whatever love he observes, except self-love. He is more than a cosmic spy. He is the accuser of God's people, the destroyer of all that is good, just, moral and right. And he is similarly described in the New Testament.

Who, then, are the "sons of God," referred to as "angels" in the NIV and other translations? This same phrase is used in Genesis

6:2 (though with a different meaning, as I argue in chapter 4 of this book), Psalm 29:1, Psalm 89:7 and Daniel 3:25.

They are called "sons"—thus they are beings that came forth from God and are in the likeness of God. They appear to serve as God's attendants or servants to do his will. One of these creatures withdrew himself from God's love and became the enemy of God and of everything that is holy, righteous and good. This one is now called Satan, because he "opposes," "resists" or "acts as an adversary" to the will of God.

This agrees with 1 Kings 22:19-22, Zechariah 3 and Revelation 12, where Satan is pictured as appearing among the good angels. Thus the whole course of redemption, described in the Bible, covers the same time in which Satan manifests his enmity to God and during which his damnation is completed. The other "sons of God" are God's angels who do his bidding and thus stand for everything opposite to Satan and his practices.

As for the testings of Job, of course it can be said that God tempts no one. But the Tempter, Satan, must receive permission from God to carry out even his work of harassment.

The book of Job is as much about God being on trial as it is about Job being tested. It was God who called Job to Satan's attention. But Satan scoffed, suggesting that Job had his reasons for serving God so faithfully. Job was a special focus of God's love and attention—that's why he served God, charged the Accuser.

Though the Lord gave Satan opportunity to do his worst, Job refused to curse God as Satan had anticipated. On that score, Satan lost badly and God was vindicated.

Job did fear and worship God "for nothing." He had not been bribed or promised a certain amount of health, wealth and prosperity if he would serve God completely, as Satan had charged. It is possible for men and women to love and fear God apart from any special benefits, or even when their circumstances are not conducive to faith. Job demonstrated that point marvelously well.

· C H A P T E R 4 5 ·

A Covenant
Not to
Lust

*I made a covenant with my eyes
not to look lustfully at a girl.*
JOB 31:1

It is commonly said that Jesus expanded or deepened the morality of the
Old Testament in his statement in the Sermon on the Mount,
"You have heard that it was said, 'Do not commit adultery.' But
I tell you that anyone who looks at a woman lustfully has already
committed adultery with her in his heart" (Mt 5:27-28).

But how can that understanding of Jesus' statement be accu-
rate, given Job's claim in Job 31:1? There must be a different
understanding of Jesus' statement or of Job's claim.

The solution to this dilemma is to note that Jesus did not
contrast what he said with what the Old Testament taught. If
one carefully notes the language of Matthew 5, it contrasts what
"you have heard" with what Jesus said.

Since our Lord is the author of the Old Testament as well as the New, it can hardly be appropriate to see the two in opposition to each other, unless we assume that God can contradict himself. Instead, what is being contrasted is the oral tradition of the Jewish community of that day with the written and personal revelation of Jesus Christ. Thus, for example, Matthew 5:43 says that conventional wisdom dictated, "Love your neighbor and hate your enemy." Nowhere in the Old Testament can one find a verse supporting the second half of that bit of advice. This confirms that the opposition Jesus set up was between what passed for truth in the public mind (some of that being correct and some of it being plain wrong) and what God wants us to know and do.

But what of Job's claim? Some contend, with a great deal of persuasive evidence, that he lived during the patriarchal age. But could a man living between 2000 to 1750 B.C. have made as high an ethical statement as Job makes here?

Job clearly was concerned about more than external behaviors. He offered daily sacrifices on behalf of all his children, for he feared that they might have sinned inwardly (Job 1:5). Here, then, was a man who thought about his own internal intentions and those of others. Can we be all that surprised to learn that he had decided to shun not only all acts of adultery but also the wrong desires that form in the eye and the heart?

Desires arising from greed, deceit and lust were taboo in this man's life. Coveting a woman was just as much sin as the act of adultery itself. Both the desire and the act were culpable before God and renounced by this Old Testament man who "feared God and shunned evil" (Job 1:1, 8; 2:3).

The point made in Job 31:1 is repeated in verses 9-12. There Job once again denies that he has been guilty of adultery; he has committed no sinful acts and has in fact restrained all the drives that could lead to such acts. He rejected all inducements to adultery.

The obligation Job laid on his eyes is consistent with warnings in other wisdom literature, in which "the eye" is seen as the source of evil impulses (Prov 6:17; 10:10; 30:17). "The eye" also is viewed as the seat of pride (Prov 30:13) and, in the Apocryphal wisdom books, as the source of sexual desire (Sirach 9:8; 26:9).

Job's claim to have made a covenant with his eyes and a determination not to look upon, or to turn his thoughts toward, an unmarried girl or another man's wife corresponds well with Ben Sirach's teaching (9:5). Moreover, Job 31:3-4 makes it clear that he expected divine retribution if he failed. Job expected that he would have to answer to God, not society, for any lapses in morality.

His covenant was no manifestation of moral heroism on his part, but a decision that was in accord with the Word of God. In fact, according to Job 31:4, Job realized that God saw everything: all of a person's ways were open before the Lord. Again, this concept of God's awareness of all a person does and thinks is echoed in other wisdom teaching (for example, Ps 33:13-15; 69:5; 94:11; 119:168; 139; Prov 5:21).

On these points there is very little difference between the moral expectations of the New Testament and those of the Old. The teaching of our Lord through Job's book and the teaching of Jesus in the Sermon on the Mount are harmonious.

The Lord Hates All Who Do Wrong and Love Violence

The arrogant cannot stand in your presence;
you hate all who do wrong.
PSALM 5:5

The LORD examines the righteous, but the wicked
and those who love violence his soul hates.
PSALM 11:5

How can a God of love and mercy be categorized as one who hates? Yet these two texts clearly affirm that he does hate wrongdoers, the wicked and all who love violence. What makes such a strong contrast possible?

Scriptural talk about God's hatred involves an idiom that does not suggest a desire of revenge. Why would God feel any need for getting even, when he is God?

Our problem with any description of God's displeasure with sin, unrighteousness or wickedness is that we define all anger as Aristotle defined it: "the desire for retaliation." With such a definition of anger goes the concept of anger and hatred of sin as a "brief madness" or "an uneasiness or discomposure of the mind, upon receipt of an injury, with the purpose of revenge." All such notions of hatred, anger and displeasure in the divine being are wide of the mark and fail to address the issues involved. Better is Lactantius' definition of anger as "a motion of the soul rousing itself to curb sin."

The problem is that anger can be dangerously close to evil when it is left unchecked and without control. Who could charge God with any of these common human faults? Thus we often object upon being told that God is angry with our sin and that he absolutely hates wrongdoing, violence and sin. Our concept of anger and our experiences with it have all too frequently involved loss of control, impulsiveness and sometimes temporary derangement. No wonder no one wants to link those kind of thoughts with God!

But God's anger toward sin is never explosive, unreasonable or unexplainable. It is never a force that controls him or a ruling passion; rather, it always remains an instrument of his will. His anger has not, therefore, shut off his compassion (Ps 77:9).

Instead, God's anger marks the end of indifference. He cannot and will not remain neutral and impassive in the presence of injustice, violence or any other sin. While God delights in doing good to his creatures (Jer 32:41) rather than expressing evil, he will unleash his anger and wrath against all sin. Yet Scripture pictures his anger as lasting only for a moment, in contrast to his love, which is much more enduring (Ps 30:5). His love remains (Jer 31:3; Hos 2:19), while his anger passes quickly (Is 26:20; 54:7-8; 57:16-19).

Passions and emotions are not in themselves evil. When kept under control, they are avenues of virtue and goodness. And our Lord is not passionless and without emotions just because he is God. In fact, this whole question of divine anger (*ira dei*) was the subject of a sharp debate in the history of the church. It became known as the question of divine passibility (that is, God's capacity to feel, suffer or become angry) versus his impassibility (imperviousness to emotion). Teachings issuing from Gnosticism (a philosophy that combined Greek and Oriental ideas with Christian teaching) forced the church to develop a doctrine of divine passibility—that God could indeed experience feelings, suffer, and be angry.

One of the gnostics, best known for his view that God never took offense, was never angry and remained entirely apathetic, was Marcion. Marcion was expelled from the church and his doctrines were anathematized in A.D. 144. Tertullian, one of the church fathers, tried to answer Marcion on this point in his work *Against Marcion*, but he unfortunately concluded that God the Father was impassible while the Son was passible and irascible—that is, able to exercise anger. Tertullian, at this point, was reflecting more of his Platonism than he was reflecting Scripture. The church had to wait until the last half of the third century before another church father, Lactantius, wrote *De ira Dei (The Anger of God)* and got the matter straightened out. For Lactantius, passions and emotions were not bad in and of themselves. What was evil was *not* being angry in the presence of sin!

God's hatred of evil is not some arbitrary force, striking where and when it wishes without any rhyme or reason. Instead, his anger against sin is measured and controlled by his love and his justice. Expressions of his outrage against the evil perpetrated on earth as well are actually signals that he continues to care deeply about us mortals and about our good.

· C H A P T E R 4 7 ·

You Will Not
Let Your Holy One
See Decay

I have set the LORD always before me.
Because he is at my right hand,
I will not be shaken.

Therefore my heart is glad and my tongue rejoices;
my body also will rest secure,
because you will not abandon me to the grave,
nor will you let your Holy One see decay.
PSALM 16:8-10

Few psalms give rise to as many important methodological and theological questions as does Psalm 16. And few passages from the Old Testament are given a more prominent place in the New Testament witness about Jesus as the Messiah. In fact, on the Day of Pentecost, Peter made Psalm 16 the showpiece in his arsenal of arguments to prove that Jesus was the expected Messiah (Acts 2:25-33).

This opinion has not, however, been shared among all Bible

scholars. Some protest that in Jewish exegesis Psalm 16 is not traditionally understood to refer to the Messiah. It does not support the contentions the apostles built upon it, argue many scholars; in particular, it does not predict the resurrection of Christ. These arguments are serious enough to warrant our considering this psalm among the hard sayings of the Old Testament.

According to its ancient title, Psalm 16 came from the hand of David. A number of phrases in the psalm contain similarities to the phraseology of other, better-known Davidic hymns.

The particular events in David's life that occasioned the writing of this psalm are not known, but three principal suggestions have been made: (1) a severe sickness, (2) a time when he was tempted to worship idols during his stay at Ziklag (2 Sam 30) and (3) his response to Nathan's prophecy about the future of his kingdom (2 Sam 7). My preference lies with the third option, since it fits best with the messianic content of the psalm.

The psalmist has experienced a time of unbounded joy and happiness, knowing that he is secure under the sovereignty of Yahweh (v. 1). The Lord himself is David's "portion" (v. 5) and his "inheritance" (v. 6). There is no good beside the Lord.

In verse 9b, the psalmist reverts to the Hebrew imperfect tense as he begins to think and talk about his future and the future of the kingdom God has given him. David will rest secure, for neither he nor God's everlasting "seed" (here called "Holy One," *hāsîd*) will be left in the grave. God has made a promise that his "seed" or "Holy One" will experience fullness of joy and pleasure in God's presence forever.

One of the most frequently asked questions is whether verse 9's reference to not being abandoned in the grave expresses the psalmist's hope for a future resurrection or his faith that God will watch over his body and spirit and preserve him from all harm on this earth.

The answer to this question hangs on the meaning and significance of the word *hāsîd*, "Holy [or Favored] One." *Hāsîd* occurs thirty-two times in the Old Testament, all in poetic texts; seventeen times it is in the plural and eleven times in the singular, and four times there are variant readings. The best way to render *hāsîd* is in the passive, "one to whom God is loyal, gracious or merciful," or better, "one in whom God manifests his grace and favor."

In Psalm 4:4[5], David claims that he is Yahweh's *hāsîd*. Likewise, Psalm 89:19-20 connects David with our term *hāsîd*: "Of all you spoke to your *hāsîd* in a vision and said: 'I have set the crown on a hero, I have exalted from the people a choice person. I have found David my servant [another messianic term] with my holy oil, and I have anointed him [a cognate term for Messiah]' " (my translation).

What else can we conclude but that David and Yahweh's "Holy One" are one and the same?

As early as Moses' era, there is a reference to "the man of your *hāsîd* whom you [Israel] tested at Massah" (Deut 33:8; see Exodus 17, where water came out of the rock at Massah as Moses struck it). The only "man" who was tested in Exodus 17:2, 7 was the Lord. Thus, *hāsîd* is clearly identified with the Lord. Hannah also spoke of the coming *hāsîd* in the phrase "the horn of his anointed" (1 Sam 2:9-10)—a concept confirmed as being messianic by Psalm 89:17-21.

The seventeen plural usages of *hāsîd* should not present any problems to this interpretation. The oscillation between the One and the many is exactly what is presented when all Israel is called the "seed" of Abraham (or one of the other men of promise), yet Christ is that "Seed" par excellence. The same phenomenon occurs with the words "anointed one," "servant" and "firstborn." Each is used in the plural as well as the singular.

Thus the apostle Peter was fully within the proper bounds of scriptural interpretation in his treatment of Psalm 16. The man

David did indeed die, but the *ḥāsîḏ* was eternal. David himself was an anointed one, but *the* Anointed One was eternal and thus the guarantee of David's confidence about the future.

David the individual went to his grave and experienced decay, but the ultimate fulfillment of Yahweh's eternal promise did not cease to exist. He experienced resurrection from the grave, just as David foresaw under the inspiration of the Spirit as he wrote Psalm 16.

My God, My God,
Why Have You
Forsaken Me?

My God, my God, why have you forsaken me?
Why are you so far from saving me,
so far from the words of my groaning?
PSALM 22:1

Psalm 22 is one of the best-known psalms because the Passion narratives
in the Gospels refer to it quite frequently. In fact, Psalm 22 was
the principal resource employed by the New Testament evangel-
ists as they attempted to portray the life, death and resurrection
of Jesus to show that he was the Messiah.

Of the thirteen (some count seventeen) major Old Testament
texts that are quoted in the Gospel narratives, nine come from
the Psalms, and five of those from Psalm 22. The best known of
them all is the cry of dereliction, "Eloi, eloi, lama sabachthani"
(Mt 27:46; Mk 15:34).

The problem is this: how do we move from the context of the
psalmist to that of our Lord? In what sense were the psalmist's

words appropriately applied to Jesus as well as to their original speaker (who probably was David, according to the psalm's ancient title)?

At first blush, the psalm does not appear to have been written as a direct prediction. In fact, some claim that the psalm actually contains nothing that its human author or its original readers would have recognized as pertaining to the Messiah.

In order to address this issue, let us first note that the psalm begins by expressing grief and suffering in what is known as the "lament" form. In verse 22, however, the lament turns into a psalm of thanksgiving and praise for the deliverance that has been experienced. Structural divisions are clearly marked by the emphatic use of certain words: "my God" and "yet you" (vv. 1, 3), "but I" (v. 6), "yet you" (v. 9) and "but you" (v. 19).

What in this text forces us to look beyond David to a messianic interpretation, as the church has done for millennia? One of the first clues is the strong adversative that comes in verse 3 with its reference to the "Holy." This adjective may function as an attribute ("Yet you are holy") or as a reference to the divine person himself, as in the NIV's "Yet you are enthroned as the Holy One."

If the second option, "Holy One" (*qadosh*), is the correct rendering, as I believe it is, then it is interesting that this Holy One is further linked with the coming Man of Promise "in [whom the] fathers [Abraham, Isaac, Jacob and others] put their trust" (v. 4). From Genesis 15:1-6 it is clear that the patriarchs did not merely put their trust in God (as simple theists); they rested their faith in the "seed" promised to Abraham (in lieu of Abraham's offer to adopt his Arab servant Eliezer). To this same Lord the psalmist turned for deliverance when he was beset by some unspecified suffering and anguish.

Yet the psalmist's suffering was merely illustrative of the suffering that would come to the Messiah. What happened to David in his position as head of the kingdom over which the Lord himself would one day reign was not without significance for the kingdom of God. To attack David's person or realm, given that he was the carrier and the earnest of the promise to be fulfilled in Christ's first and second comings, was ultimately to attack God's Son and his kingdom.

Small wonder, then, that this psalm was on Jesus' mind as he hung on the cross. The so-called fourth word from the cross, "My God, my God, why have you forsaken me?" and the sixth word, "It is finished," come from the first and last verses of this psalm. Not only is the first verse quoted in two Gospels, but verses 7-8 are clearly alluded to in Matthew 27:39, 43; verse 18 is quoted directly in John 19:24 and in part in Matthew 27:35, Mark 15:24 and Luke 23:34; and verse 22 is quoted directly in Hebrews 2:12. The final verse, 31, is cited, in part, in John 19:30. No wonder this psalm has been called "the Fifth Gospel."

We conclude that the God in whom David's forefathers trusted—the Man of Promise, the Messiah—is the same one to whom David now entrusts his life as he experiences savage attacks. And those attacks were only a foreshadowing of what the Messiah himself would one day face.

But there is really no despair or hand-wringing here. Triumph was certain; the dominion of the coming one would be realized (v. 28). Just as God sat down and rested at the conclusion of creation, there would be a day when the Lord would cry, "It is finished!" as redemption was completed. Yet even this would be only a foretaste of the final shout of triumph in Revelation 21:6 over the fulfillment of the new heavens and new earth: "It is done."

John Calvin observed, "From the tenor of the whole [psalm], it appears that David does not here refer merely to one persecution, but comprehends all the persecutions which he suffered under Saul."[1] Though that is doubtless true, under the inspiration of the Holy Spirit David went beyond the boundaries of all his own sufferings as he pictured the one who would suffer an even greater agony.

Yes, David did see the sufferings of that final one who would come in his life; but he also saw that the Messiah would emerge victorious, with a kingdom that would never fail.

Note

[1]John Calvin, *Commentary on Psalms* (Edinburgh: T. & T. Clark, 1845), 1:357.

• C H A P T E R 4 9 •

Your Throne, O God, Will Last Forever

Your throne, O God, will last for ever and ever;
a scepter of justice will be the scepter of your kingdom.
PSALM 45:6

Psalm 45:6 represents one of the most famous cruces interpretum to be found in the Old Testament. How are the words "your throne, O God" to be understood? In what sense could any mortal's throne be connected with deity? And if it is a statement that applies to divinity, then in what sense can it apply to any earthly throne? One way or another, we are caught in a trap.

Not a few scholars, daunted by what they consider to be insuperable difficulties with the text as it stands, have suggested a long list of emendations to that text, yet without any manuscripts to warrant such revisions and with no consensus of opinion among the learned community.

It is clear that the ancient versions uniformly treat *Elohim*, "God," as a vocative (that is, as a noun of address—"O God" as found in the NIV), even though it has no article attached to the divine name. *Elohim* appears as a vocative with the presence of the article only once (Judg 16:28), but in fifty other cases of the vocative of God's name, there is no article present in the Hebrew.

Translators have been forced to concede that they must deal with the words that are before us in the Hebrew text. But since this phrase appears in such a succinct form of Hebrew poetry, at least five different ways of interpreting this phrase have been set forth.[1]

The Revised Standard Version adopts a genitival relationship, suggesting possession or source: "Your throne of God," that is, "the throne God has given you" or "the throne established and protected by God." Yet this will not work, since the word *throne* has two different kinds of genitives or possessives—a construction without parallels in the rest of the Old Testament.

R. A. Knox's rendering, "God is the support of your throne," is grammatically possible (as it uses Elohim either as a subject or a predicate, with the idea that God is the creator or sustainer of the king's rule), but it runs into conceptual problems. Even in a book where bold metaphors are used, the concepts of God and of a throne are much too dissimilar to permit their easy linkage. How could any human throne belong to the category of divine beings ("is God")? Furthermore, it is unlikely that words like "is founded by," "is protected by," "is the support of" or "has divine qualities" can be extracted from the single Hebrew word *Elohim*.

A third rendition cavalierly adds the word "throne" a second time: "Your throne is God's throne," or "Your throne will be a divine throne." There is nothing wrong, of course, with the concept that a royal throne could belong to God, for that is expressed in 1 Chronicles 29:23 (see also 28:5; 1 Kings 3:28), where Solomon is described as sitting "on the throne of Yahweh." But the problem once again is conceptual rather than grammatical. In those instances generally cited in support of this translation, such as "its walls [were walls of] wood" (Ezek 41:22), there is an implied identity between the subject and the predicate. The second noun denotes the material of which the an object was made or a characteristic it possessed. But God is neither the material of which the throne is made nor a characteristic it possesses.

The New English Bible renders this phrase "Your throne is like God's throne." But such a translation must assume the conflation of two idioms in Psalm 45:6, which are otherwise unattested anywhere else in the Old Testament. There are just too many words added to the text without foundation.

The best translation, and the one that has been supported by all the ancient versions, is "Your throne, O God." The King James Version, the Revised Version, the Revised Standard Version margin, the New American Standard Bible, the New American Bible, the Jerusalem Bible, the New International Version, Knox, and the Berkeley translation all translate the Hebrew in this way, as do many modern commentators.

To whom, then, does *Elohim* refer? The king was not regarded as the incarnation of deity. Rather, he was "Yahweh's anointed" and served as the Lord's deputy on earth. This was particularly true of David, who stood in the promised line of the Messiah. He had been adopted as God's "son" in 2 Samuel 7:14 (see also Ps 2:7; 89:26).

Yet he was more than merely elected by God. Since he was endowed with the Spirit of Yahweh, he exhibited certain characteristics that foreshadowed the coming divine rule and reign of the greater David, Christ Jesus. While allowance must be made for hyperbolic language in some of these psalms and in the ancient Near Eastern court, the court and throne given to David and his descendants are described in terms that suggest they exceed anything known previously, or since.

However, lest we start attributing qualities of deity to mere mortals and not to the office, dynasty and kingdom that they represented, verse 7 reminds us that the extraordinary use of *Elohim* in verse 6 is not without qualification. Yahweh was the king's God; the king was not his own God! "Therefore God, your God, has set you above your companions by anointing you with the oil of joy," declares the psalmist with care.

The rendering "Your throne, O God" is the most defensible and most satisfactory solution of all. King David is addressed as Elohim, but it was because of the promise he carried in his person from God, because of his office, his dynasty and the kingdom he had received as an inauguration of the final kingdom of God to which the Messiah would one day lay total claim.

Note

[1]See Murray Harris, "Elohim in Psalm 45," *Tyndale Bulletin* 35 (1984):65-89, for a detailed discussion of these alternatives.

· C H A P T E R 5 0 ·

Do Not Take Your Holy Spirit from Me

*Do not cast me from your presence
or take your Holy Spirit from me.
Restore to me the joy of your salvation
and grant me a willing spirit, to sustain me.*
PSALM 51:11-12

Are we to suppose that Psalm 51's "Holy Spirit" is the same Holy Spirit to which the New Testament refers? Or is an understanding of the Holy Spirit too advanced for the state of revelation under the older covenant?

Few doctrines suffer more from neglect of the Old Testament data than the doctrine of the Holy Spirit. Even those scholars who do consider some of the Old Testament evidence quickly summarize it and use it merely as a jumping-off point to address the main pieces of evidence, which are assumed to be in the New Testament.

However, if that is so, why is it that Jesus expected Nicodemus, in John 3, to know about the person and work of the Holy Spirit? Where could this "teacher of the Jews" have gained such a doctrine if the Old Testament has such a paucity of teaching on this theme? Should Jesus have "marveled" that Nicodemus was so deficient in his understanding of pneumatology in the Old Testament, when our own generation probably could hardly do better?

Some of the reasons for this paucity of information are fairly obvious. To mention the most obvious factor, there are only three uses of the complete expression "Holy Spirit" in the Old Testament: Psalm 51:11 and Isaiah 63:10 and 11. The most common Hebrew term is *rwh*, appearing 378 times and translated variously as "wind," "spirit," "direction," "side" and some half-dozen other words.

It is the three major prophets who use the word *spirit* most often. The term *rwh* appears fifty-two times in Ezekiel, fifty-one times in Isaiah and eighteen in Jeremiah. Particularly important is Ezekiel 37:1-14, which portrays the life-giving power of God's Spirit in this description of the Valley of Dry Bones. Only the Spirit of God can put life and spirit back into a nation, such as Israel, that had passed out of existence.

What, then, was the operation of the Holy Spirit in the Old Testament? Did the Spirit in the old covenant come upon persons for a short period of time for a special task, while in the New Testament he indwelt the believer, as some have argued? If so, this assumes that the saints of the older covenant became members of the family of God merely by observing the rules and regulations of the Torah. But how could that be true in light of Jesus's stern rebuke to Nicodemus, an event still prior to the cross and one that demanded a knowledge of the Spirit from the Old Testament alone? And how can that be made to square with the Old Testament's demand for a heart religion—Jeremiah's "circumcision of the heart" rather than a mere circumcision of the flesh?

What did Ezekiel mean when, in chapter 36, he pressed the necessity of a new heart and a new spirit, which was probably the chapter that Jesus held Nicodemus responsible for? The Old Testament does teach of a personal Holy Spirit who brought people to faith in the Man of Promise who was to come in the line of Abraham and David—and the Spirit indwelt those saints just as surely as he indwelt believers in the New Testament.

In Psalm 51:11, David confessed his sin with Bathsheba. His desire was to have a clean heart and spirit before God. He fears that God might withdraw the indwelling presence and work of his Holy Spirit from him. What David desired was a "steadfast spirit" (v. 10) to be renewed within him. He feared the removal of God's Holy Spirit, because he had drifted away from God as a result of his sin and decision to ride it out while Bathsheba's pregnancy was in progress. At last he had confessed his sin, and now he found himself in deep spiritual hunger and desiring to be reconciled with God.

Some will object, "If the Old Testament believer already possessed the Holy Spirit, why was Pentecost necessary?" George Smeaton gave the best answer to that question when he affirmed, "[The Holy Spirit] must have a coming in state, in a solemn and visible manner, accompanied with visible effects as well as Christ had and whereof all the Jews should be, and were, witnesses."[1] Pentecost signaled a visible and mightier-than-ever manifestation of the person and work of the Holy Spirit. (See Joel 2:28; it was a "downpour" of the Spirit compared to the previous showers.) This was the inception of the *full* experience of the Holy Spirit. After all, the Holy Spirit, like the Father and Son, had existed from all eternity. He did not remain bound and without assignment in the older era. But Pentecost did mark a fuller realization of what had been already in progress.

Some will rightfully call to mind certain New Testament texts that seem to imply that the Holy Spirit's coming to indwell the believer is a brand-new feature of the gospel era. Especially relevant are John 7:37-39, 14:16-17 and 16:7.[2]

Most will agree that in John 3:5-10, Jesus himself suggested that the Holy Spirit was operating in bringing salvation prior to Christ's death on the cross. When Jesus taught his disciples how to pray, he said, "If you . . . know how to give good gifts to your children, how much more will your Father in heaven give the Holy Spirit to those who ask him!" (Lk 11:13). Apparently, that gift was already available, even before Pentecost.

Of all the texts cited in this debate, the most important is John 14:17: "You know him, for he lives with *[para]* you and *is* in you." There is a strong manuscript tradition for reading the present tense of the verb *to be* ("is") rather than the future tense ("will be"). The two forms, *estai* and *esti,* are very easily confused, but the present tense appears, as B. F. Westcott concludes, to be less like a correction and probably represents the more difficult reading. (Textual critics adhere to the principle of choosing the "more difficult" reading, since copiers of the text tended to "correct" the text to the simpler or more expected reading.) Thus the Holy Spirit already was with the Old Testament believer and present in all who believed.

We conclude that the Holy Spirit did bring new life to those who believed under the old covenant and that he personally indwelt them. But just as Calvary was necessary, even though Jesus' life and work were anticipated in the Old Testament, Pentecost was necessary even though the benefits of the Holy Spirit's work were already present in the Old Testament.

That is why David feared the possible loss of the Holy Spirit. Even if one of the ministries of the Holy Spirit was the gift of government—a gift that had been given to and then taken away from his predecessor King Saul—David appears to have been worried about more than the loss of his ability to govern in Jerusalem. He feared losing the indwelling comfort and help of the Paraclete himself. That would be tantamount to standing outside the presence of God.

Notes

[1]George Smeaton, *The Doctrine of the Holy Spirit*, 2d ed. (Edinburgh: T. & T. Clark, 1889), p. 49.
[2]For a fuller discussion of this point, see Walter C. Kaiser, Jr., *Toward Rediscovering the Old Testament* (Grand Rapids: Zondervan, 1987), pp. 135-41.

God Does Not Delight in Sacrifices

You do not delight in sacrifice, or I would bring it;
you do not take pleasure in burnt offerings.
The sacrifices of God are a broken spirit;
a broken and contrite heart, O God, you will not despise. . . .
Then there will be righteous sacrifices,
whole burnt offerings to delight you;
then bulls will be offered on your altar.
PSALM 51:16-17, 19

It is startling to read in Psalm 51 that God does not wish worshipers to bring any sacrifices. When one considers the extensive instructions to the contrary in the book of Leviticus, what could the psalmist have had in mind except what appears to be a flat-out contradiction? Hadn't God issued a command that sacrifices were to be brought to his house?

This text is not alone in posing this problem. A number of other texts appear to teach the same disavowal of sacrifices. Some of them are 1 Samuel 15:14-15, 22;[1] Jeremiah 7:21-23;

Hosea 6:6; Micah 6:6-8; and Zechariah 7:4-7. In each of these texts, God appears to be spurning the external acts and rituals of worship, usually as expressed in sacrifices. But we will be mistaken if we assume that this is an absolute rejection of the acts of worship he had previously required under the Mosaic covenant.

Some have sought to relieve the tension produced by texts such as this one by saying that the instructions for the sacrifices came later; they were not, as a prima-facie reading of the text would suggest and as most conservative scholars have assumed, from the hand of Moses. However, we regard this solution as too high a price to pay for a quick harmonization of the data. If the Law had come later (in the fifth century B.C.), surely the writers, or even their editors and redactors (if such were involved), would not have been careless enough to ignore the fact that they had created a problem in the text. There must have been some other solution that was apparent to and understood by those earlier audiences.

We believe that solution is to be found in the Old Testament writers' constant pleading for the worshiper's heart attitude to be set right. That is the precise point of these verses from Psalm 51 as well.

What was the use of piling on sacrifices if they were not expressions of a spirit of contrition and genuine piety of life? God always inspects the giver, even in the Old Testament (see the discussion in chapter 1 of this volume), before he inspects the gift, offering or praise. How can one who is unclean offer a clean sacrifice?

Psalm 51:16's statement of denial is qualified by what follows in verse 17. The sacrifices of a broken and contrite spirit are the gifts God seeks as a prelude to any sacrifices of sheep, goats or bulls. One whose heart is repentant is never despised by God. Consequently, the sacrifices from such a one are prized.

Verse 19 concludes with the position we have been arguing for here. *"Then,"* says the Hebrew text in a most emphatic tone, "you will be pleased with the sacrifices of the righteous and whole burnt offerings, then they will offer on your altar bulls" (my literal translation).

The difficulty of these verses is not to be solved in the manner once fashionable (by late-dating the Law to the fifth or fourth century B.C.), but by noticing the constant urging of God's servants that the people give their hearts and their lives in deep contrition and brokenness of spirit before they observe feasts, fasts, Sabbaths, or sacrifices.

Isaiah, for example, demanded that the people stop their sacrifices, convocations, appointed feast days and prayers (Is 1:11-15); instead, he said, they must begin by coming before God with clean hands and a clean heart. If only the Israelites would first come and reason with the Lord, even if their sins were as red as crimson, they could be as white as wool; they had only to be obedient and willing (Is 1:16-18). Then God could accept their sacrifices, just as he accepted David's sacrifices for his sin with Bathsheba *after* David repented. Rote religion can never substitute for purity of heart.

This teaching is repeated so many times in the Old Testament, as well as in the New, that we marvel that scholars—not to mention many contemporary lay readers of the Bible—continue to miss it. God has not changed his order of priorities in all these years.

Note

[1]On this text, see Walter C. Kaiser, Jr., *Hard Sayings of the Old Testament* (Downers Grove, Ill.: InterVarsity Press, 1988), pp. 110-12.

· C H A P T E R 5 2 ·

The Prosperity of the Wicked

Surely God is good to Israel,
to those who are pure in heart.
But as for me, my feet had almost slipped;
I had nearly lost my foothold.
For I envied the arrogant
when I saw the prosperity of the wicked . . .
till I entered the sanctuary of God;
then I understood their final destiny.
PSALM 73:1-3, 17

Psalm 73 deals with a problem that has often perplexed God's people. Actually, it is a twofold problem whose parts are interrelated: why must the godly suffer so frequently, and why do the ungodly seem to be so prosperous?

Psalm 73 is one of the classic statements of this two-pronged question. In fact, so open is the psalmist about his own doubts that he allows us to penetrate deep into his inner being as he leads us to the very brink of despair over this most grievous problem. But he recovers just in the nick of time; in verse 17 he reorders his thinking about this problem and thus saves himself, and those of us who read his psalm, from falling over the precipice of despair. Like a number of other psalms, this one begins with the conclusion. The resolution of the problem ultimately comes not from a particular apologetic approach, but from the contemplation of the goodness of God (v. 1).

The steps by which the psalmist, Asaph, arrived at the conclusion that God is good are also important. Having started out right, he went astray as he looked around, but then he came back to God again. The difficulty is in how he came back: his journey almost led him into disaster.

Asaph has given us a most memorable picture of what the world calls successful people: their position in life ("they have no struggles"), their health ("their bodies are healthy and strong"), their responsibilities ("they are free from the burdens common to man"), their arrogance ("pride is their necklace; they clothe themselves with violence") and their insensitivity to evil ("from their callous hearts comes iniquity").

As if all of this were not enough, the psalmist heard these proud, wealthy, healthy people boast, "How can God know? Does the Most High have knowledge?" (v. 11). Such blasphemy! "We don't care what you say about God," these folks boast. "We are doing just fine without him or his help! Nothing goes wrong for us; look at some of you who claim God exists. If he does, then why are you not being helped? Why aren't you doing at least as well as we are?"

Such taunts are galling and hard to swallow. But let it be said that being perplexed or having doubts over this problem is not a sin; what is a sin is to forget God's goodness and what we have learned in God's house about the end of all such boasters. That would be to take the short view of a problem that must be considered over the long haul.

The "now generation" demands a quick resolution of all problems, no matter how knotty, on the basis of data immediately at hand. Though jumping to conclusions satisfies the desire for speedy resolution, it ultimately leads to envy (v. 3) and depression (v. 16).

In order to get understanding, Asaph went into the sanctuary of God. Religion is not the opiate of the people; it is supposed to bring understanding (v. 17). Such understanding can help us gain our footing once again.

What the prosperous, healthy, arrogant people do not realize is that they are standing "on slippery ground" (v 18). They are not as free as they think themselves to be. And all that they have is temporary, on loan from God.

Over against this precarious position rests the steadfast goodness of God, who holds his own by the hand (v. 23) and guides them (v. 24). "Afterward [he] will take [us] into glory" (v. 24).

The problem of the prosperity of the wicked and the suffering of believers is to be resolved in the goodness of the God who personally walks and talks with his own and who will ultimately bring us to be with him in glory. Contrariwise, the prosperity of the wicked is very short-lived when judged from God's perspective. It is *their* feet that are on a slippery slope, not the believers'. Those who believe are gaining understanding of God's goodness as they approach God's house.

The wicked often do prosper—at least for the moment; but the righteous shall endure forever. And the righteous will always experience the goodness of God.

God Crushed the Heads of Leviathan

But you, O God, are my king from of old;
you bring salvation upon the earth.
It was you who split open the sea by your power;
you broke the heads of the monster in the waters.
It was you who crushed the heads of Leviathan
and gave him as food to the creatures of the desert.
PSALM 74:12-14

It is not unusual, of course, to find imagery used in the Bible, especially in biblical poetry. But when that imagery seems to make use of mythological allusions, as does Psalm 74, we may wonder what it means. Is the Bible implying the reality of the mythological world? Or perhaps the imagery was already remote in time and function from its original connotations, so that the psalmist used it as casually as we use mythological names for the days of the week and for certain holidays, such as Easter.

In Psalm 74, the psalmist is attempting to convince God that he should intervene on behalf of his city Jerusalem, just as he had done in his victory over evil—perhaps, as some think, at the creation of the universe.

As he makes his appeal, the poet adopts language parallel to that used in mythical texts from Ugarit (a Canaanite language whose vocabulary and spelling are similar to those of Hebrew). God "split open the sea" (in Hebrew and Ugaritic, *yam)*. Heavily influenced by the Ugaritic mythological parallels, many modern scholars assume that the allusion to splitting (or "dividing") refers to some primordial powers. But actually it refers to the division of the Red Sea (or better, "Reed Sea") at the exodus. The name for "sea" is *yam* in Hebrew and Ugaritic, and thus the real and the mythological share the same word. Only context and usage can determine the difference.

Given the context of Psalm 74, however, with its references to multiple heads and to Leviathan, it may well be that the poet has borrowed the terms from their Canaanite and mythological background without in any way endorsing the myth. If God could part the waters at the exodus, think of what he could do for Israel in this time of need! This is the psalmist's point.

In verse 13, God also is said to have "broke[n] the heads of Tannim," another name for "sea" *(yam)*. According to the Ugaritic text 67:3 (approximately 1400 B.C.), this monster had seven heads. Earlier Mesopotamian cylinder seals depict seven-headed dragons being attacked by the gods of that land.

God also "crushed the heads of Leviathan" (v. 14). Leviathan appears only six times in the Old Testament, often as a figure for Egypt. In Ugaritic, this monster was known under the name of Lotan, but it appears here in Psalm 74:13-14 with other beasts such as Yam and Tannin (Tannim).

If Leviathan must be made to correspond with a known creature, then the large aquatic animal known as the crocodile (Job 41) would probably be correct. Leviathan swims in God's great and wide sea (Ps 104:25-26). He has a scaly hide (Job 41:7, 15-

17), with terrible teeth (Job 41:14).

Now whether the multiheaded Leviathan of Psalm 74 is one of the mythological creatures or a name from old myths for the contemporary crocodile is difficult to say. If the imagery is not from pagan sources, then the references to the "heads of Leviathan" may well be a historical allusion, an image for the corpses of the Egyptian troops that washed ashore after the Reed Sea closed over them.

I lean toward the view that these are words that originally had mythological associations, but in their biblical context have been purged of all such overtones. They now function as words of hyperbolic force to suggest the kinds of powers that God is capable of dealing with, and they particularly remind us of God's marvelous deliverance at the exodus and the Reed Sea.

Thus, the Bible makes reference to these images from the dead world of myth without giving the slightest hint of belief in any such mythology.[1]

Note

[1]For more examples of biblical use of such imagery, see Elmer B. Smick, "Mythology and the Book of Job," *Journal of the Evangelical Theological Society* 13 (1970):101-8.

Drink Water from Your Own Cistern

Drink water from your own cistern,
running water from your own well.
Should your springs overflow in the streets,
your streams of water in the public squares?
Let them be yours alone,
never to be shared with strangers.
May your fountain be blessed,
and may you rejoice in the wife of your youth.
A loving doe, a graceful deer—
may her breasts satisfy you always,
may you ever be captivated by her love.
Why be captivated, my son, by an adulteress?
Why embrace the bosom of another man's wife?
For a man's ways are in full view of the LORD,
and he examines all his paths.
PROVERBS 5:15-21

Proverbs 5:15-21 *is usually classified as an allegory. As such, it bears* the same relationship to a metaphor that a parable and a simile share. Parables use words in their natural sense, while allegories use words metaphorically. The temptation in interpreting allegories is to overinterpret, finding too many minute meanings by making all the details of the imagery significant in and of themselves.

Proverbs 5 appears to be talking about the conservation of water. But then we are baffled by verse 17's assertion that water should be for oneself, not shared with strangers. Why would the writer suddenly express such a selfish attitude about sharing water from his well?

When verse 18 intrusively interjects "and may you rejoice in the wife of your youth," it is our first real clue that this may be an allegory whose point is not the conservation of water.

One of the rules for interpreting allegories is to note the context. The entire first part of this chapter is a warning against the loose woman. Given that context, along with this reference to rejoicing in the wife of one's youth, it slowly dawns on us that what is being extolled in this allegory is the enjoyment and fidelity of marital love over against illicit intercourse. That teaching is strikingly brought out in verse 19, where one's own marriage mate is described as "a loving doe, a graceful deer"—a most appropriate pair of metaphors for the beauty found in one's own wife as opposed to the adulterous woman depicted in the earlier part of the chapter.

But what about the particulars in the interpretation of this beautiful allegory (which was probably written by Solomon and serves as an introduction to the themes of the Song of Songs)? Five different words or phrases are used here for the source of water: *cistern, well, springs, streams of water* and *fountain*. Attempts to isolate some special metaphorical meaning in each and every one of these terms would prove fruitless. Remember, we must not try to make everything in the allegory a symbol of something else. In any case, the form of Hebrew parallelism used with these terms assures us that different meanings are not intended; these are synonymous terms used for the sake of variety and effect.

The wife is a cistern, well, spring, stream or fountain because she is able to satisfy the desire of her husband. In the ancient Near East, a spring on one's property was regarded as very valuable and significant.

The idea, then, is this: be content with marital relations with your own wife. Find your delight and satisfaction in her rather than going elsewhere to taste the wells and springs of others. Faithfulness to your own wife is so natural and so pleasant that the question must be asked, Why would you ever be attracted to anyone else? What is more, remember that all of your life is directly viewed by God—and that includes the bedroom!

Some confusion has existed over whether verse 16 should be translated in the affirmative ("Your springs will overflow in the streets"), the imperative ("Let your springs overflow in the streets") or the interrogative ("Should your springs overflow in the streets?"). Some, believing that the affirmative and imperative renderings made the writer contradict himself, inserted a negative particle in the text, but this was without any warrant from preserved Hebrew texts. Those who adopted the affirmative and imperative renderings understood them to indicate numerous progeny. But this concept of the passage breaks the unity of the image of marital fidelity and does not fit with verse 17.

All these difficulties are avoided if we take verse 16 as an interrogative. The meaning, then, would be, "Why would you let your wife go about the streets as a harlot? On the contrary, let her be for yourself only, and not for strangers. Likewise, the husband should drink from his own well. His wife should be the only person to satisfy him."

The Scriptures do much to foster marital fidelity and to lift high this loyalty as the best road to fulfillment and happiness. In fact, the Lord continues to inspect all of a person's ways, for everything is open and plain before the God who has called us to be holy to him and faithful to our marriage vows.

Rescue Those Being Led Away to Death

Rescue those being led away to death;
hold back those staggering toward slaughter.
If you say, "But we knew nothing about this,"
does not he who weighs the heart perceive it?
Does not he who guards your life know it?
Will he not repay each person according to what he has done?
PROVERBS 24:11-12

T his text had remained largely unnoticed until it came into national prominence as a theme verse to ground Operation Rescue's project of blocking access to abortion clinics. The question we must pose, then, is this: Does this text provide grounds for actively opposing those who are involved in evil?

These two verses belong to a section of Proverbs (22:17—24:22) that shares many similarities with the Egyptian wisdom piece known as *Instruction of Amenemope*. Whether the Egyptian book is dependent on the biblical book of Proverbs, as Robert Oliver Kevin has argued,[1] or the book of Proverbs is dependent to some degree on the Egyptian work, as Adolf Erman argued in 1924 in a German work, or both Proverbs and the Egyptian piece are dependent on a third unknown Semitic source, as argued by W. O. E. Oesterley,[2] is too difficult to say based on the evidence at hand. The Egyptian work had some thirty "chapters" or sayings. Given that the Hebrew text of Proverbs does not organize its collection according to this scheme, it is difficult to avoid the question of 22:20, "Have I not written thirty sayings for you . . . ?" Following such a scheme, on purely hypothetical and internal grounds some have divided these verses into twenty-five sayings.

It would appear that this text warns against negligence and a general lack of concern for those of our neighbors who are threatened with danger. Since the particular danger is not defined in this passage, we must infer that the warning applies to all cases of our neighbors' danger.

Two literal demands are made here: rescue the person who is in prison awaiting death, and also rescue the person on the way to execution. But this presumes that those whose life is threatened are innocent and have been condemned unjustly.

Some take the words *death* and *slaughter* to be metaphors for the oppression of the poor. Nothing in the text, however, supports a metaphorical interpretation.

According to verse 12, to claim that one was unaware of the issues or the consequences is not adequate to negate one's responsibility to help. In fact, verse 12 strengthens the religious character of the call to action in verse 11. Disclaimers and feigned ignorance will not divert from us the eye and gaze of God. Surely he knows what is right and wrong, and what we could and could not have done. To whine that it was no business of ours, when we were in the presence of wrong, will not satisfy the Judge of the universe. God will weigh our hearts—not like the Egyptian god of wisdom, Thot, who allegedly placed the heart of an individual on one side of a scale and a feather of truth on the other side, to see whether the hearts of Egyptians were true or false—but with the righteousness of his own divine character and the witness of his all-seeing eyes.

These texts do call for an active involvement where we might have wished to excuse ourselves. Whether it authorizes all "rescue" actions is a question that goes beyond our purview here. It certainly does not mean that believers should become vigilantes, taking the law into their own hands, or opposing the state because they think it is evil. But there will come times when we must take a stand and do all that is rightfully within our power to rescue the one who has been left bereft of scriptural justice.

Notes

[1]Robert Oliver Kevin, "The Wisdom of Amen-em-apt and Its Possible Dependence upon the Book of Proverbs," *Journal of the Society for Oriental Research* **14** (1930):115-57.

[2]W. O. E. Oesterley, "The 'Teaching of Amen-em-Ope' and the Old Testament," *Zeitschrift für alttestamentliche Wissenschaft* **45** (1927):9-24.

· C H A P T E R 5 6 ·

Give Beer
to Those Who
Are Perishing

*Give beer to those who are perishing,
wine to those who are in anguish;
let them drink and forget their poverty
and remember their misery no more.*
PROVERBS 31:6-7

S ome have been startled by these two verses and have had trouble fitting them with the rest of scriptural teaching. The problem here is to determine who are those who are "perishing" and "in anguish." And why do they need a drink to lessen the pain of their misery and to help them forget their poverty? The reference is cryptic, to say the least.

If we are to construct a response, these two verses must be set in their larger teaching group of verses. At the very minimum, the section comprises verses 4-7 of Proverbs 31. A contrast is set up between kings, who are advised against drinking lest they be incapable of responding justly when the oppressed come to them for legal relief, and those who are perishing and who carry no responsibilities such as the king carries.

Thus this proverb begins by warning us that wine and beer could cause the king to compromise his integrity. If the king were to become addicted to alcohol to escape the rigors of his office and the burdens of his responsibilities, he would be expressing cowardice, a loss of nerve for the tasks set before him (vv. 4-5). A drinking sovereign would have his vitality sapped; his mind would not be clear, but unpredictable, irresponsible and inconsistent.

On the other hand, the king is urged to give wine and beer to those who need respite from the intolerable weight of their burdens. Whether these individuals were only criminals who had been condemned to die or whether a much larger group is meant cannot be determined from this text.

It is true that condemned convicts were given a potion just prior to their execution. Perhaps it was on the grounds of this proverb that the noblewomen of Jerusalem prepared a sop for Jesus as he hung on the cross, but Jesus rejected it, apparently because he wished to be sensitive to the pain for which he was giving his life (Mk 15:23; also note the Talmud: Sanhedrin 43a).

All who have read the Bible carefully are quite aware that it makes a case for moderation, not total abstinence. It is only because of the failure of many to control their drinking that many believers have advocated total abstinence; they are objecting to the large numbers of people who are abused, injured or killed each year as a result of drunkenness. Alcohol abuse has become a major moral problem in our day, and more than Mothers Against Drunk Driving should be protesting the carnage that takes place on our highways.

Yet there is the other side of the coin for those who are able to be moderate in their alcoholic intake: wine can make the heart happy (Ps 104:15) and lift one's spirits above sorrow and poverty.

But lest Proverbs 31:6-7 be viewed as emphatically endorsing the use for alcohol for those who are poor and miserable, it must be remembered that the proverb aims at making a comparative judgment, not an absolute one. Ordinary men and women may drink sometimes to forget their poverty and their perplexities; the king, on the other hand, would be in danger of forgetting the law and cheating those who needed help if he adopted a similar lifestyle. The proverb is more concerned about drunken kings than it is about giving instructions for the general populace.

Furthermore, it must be kept in mind that those who are contrasted with the king may well be prisoners on death row who need something to assuage their terror in the final moments before the state takes their life in punishment for some serious crime.

• C H A P T E R 5 7 •

God Will Bring Every Deed into Judgment

Now all has been heard;
here is the conclusion of the matter:
Fear God and keep his commandments,
for this is the whole duty of man.
For God will bring every deed into judgment,
including every hidden thing,
whether it is good or evil.
ECCLESIASTES 12:13-14

Many modern readers of the book of Ecclesiastes cannot believe that the book originally ended on such a high ethical and theological note. Therefore, the conventional wisdom of many scholars is to attribute these final verses of the book to a late manuscript addition intended to ensure that the book would be adopted into the canon of Scriptures.

Could a book that could very well have come from the hand of Solomon have been capable of such elevated theology as to conclude that fearing God was the main task of men and women and that obeying God was the most excellent way? Could it argue that one day each person would give an account of all he or she had done in life before God, from whom it was impossible to hide anything? That is the issue here, and what an issue it is! First, we must note that there is no manuscript evidence to suggest that this alleged pious ending was dropped into place by some late redactor wanting to make sure Ecclesiastes remained in the scriptural canon. All available manuscripts reflect our present ending, so the supposition of its being an addition must remain just that: a supposition.

On the other hand, this brief text might well supply one of the keys for understanding the book, for it purports to be the summary of the whole book. I have argued for this view elsewhere.[1]

The warning that everything done on earth is reviewable in the final day was not meant to scare people, but to put a holy restraint in them. If God will judge all these acts, then it would follow that those being judged are capable of being resurrected, or at least able to appear personally and consciously before the living Lord for his verdict. The implication is that death is not a final end for the author of this book—though many who have studied Ecclesiastes have assumed that it is.

Injustice in this world is so objectionable that God has provided avenues for immediate amelioration of wrongdoing through human courts of law. However, final relief must come in the future, when the ultimate Judge, the Lord himself, comes to rectify all wrong. This theme of the need for a final judgment is raised several times in the course of the book (Eccles 3:17; 9:1; 11:9), as well as in the conclusion in 12:14. Obviously, the "Preacher" believes in a judgment after death and expects that all that has not been set right on earth will be set right in that day by God.

This interpretation of the last two verses is in harmony with the rest of the epilog (Eccles 12:8-14). Our writer concludes by restating the theme he had announced in 1:2: " 'Meaningless! Meaningless!' says the Teacher. 'Everything is meaningless.' " In other words, how futile it is to have lived life without having known the key to life.

But that is not the end of the matter; the writer has a solution. He quickly adds his qualifications for giving such heady advice in 12:9-10. He laid claim, by virtue of revelation, to being "wise"; therefore, he "continually taught the people knowledge" with a caring attitude and a deliberateness that elicited his audience's serious attention.

His words were "pleasant" ones or "words of grace." His was not a haphazard spouting of negativisms, nihilisms or an eat-drink-and-be-merry philosophy. Rather, he taught "right words . . . upright and true." Any interpreter of this book who fails to take these claims seriously is not listening patiently enough to what is being said. So useful are the words of this whole book that they can be used as goads to proper action or as nails on which you can hang your hat (v. 11). These teachings are not experiential or autobiographical; they come from "the one Shepherd." This can be no one but the Shepherd of Israel (Ps 80:1), the Shepherd of Psalm 23:1. The ideas in Ecclesiastes do not come from cynicism, skepticism or worldly wisdom, but from the Shepherd.

The grand conclusion to this book is that we are to fear the Living God and heed his Word. This is no legalistic formula, but a path for happiness. In coming to know God we come to know ourselves, for believing faith opens us up to the riches of the treasures of God, humankind and the world.

Since God is a living being and since men and women live forever, every deed, even what has been secret, is reviewable in that final day by the Lord who knows us so well. The apostle Paul echoes this teaching in 2 Corinthians 5:10. Humans are responsible beings, and one day each will personally face the Lord to give an account of the deeds done in the flesh.

Note

[1]Walter C. Kaiser, Jr., *Ecclesiastes: Total Life* (Chicago: Moody, 1978).

· C H A P T E R 5 8 ·

Love Is
As Strong
As Death

Place me like a seal over your heart,
like a seal on your arm;
for love is as strong as death,
its jealousy unyielding as the grave.
It burns like blazing fire,
like the very flame of the LORD.
Many waters cannot quench love;
rivers cannot wash it away.
If one were to give
all the wealth of his house for love,
it would be utterly scorned.
SONG OF SONGS 8:6-7

Song of Songs has long been a closed book to many people because of the difficulty they have had in interpreting it. If the book is teaching on what true marital love is all about from a divine perspective, which is certainly what it seems to be, why is the chief character Solomon? Most of us hardly consider Solomon a paragon of monogamous marriage!

Furthermore, where do we find the proper key to make a good

entry into the book? Is there any place where the narrative, play, drama or poem (whichever it really is) comes to some kind of focus and gives the reader a clue for properly understanding the book?

The answer, I believe, is to be found in Song of Songs 8:6-7. The pronominal suffixes of the Hebrew text are all clearly masculine from the end of verse 5 to verse 7; hence the speaker here is the Shulamite maiden. She is addressing her beloved one, the man to whom she has sung praises and whom she has courted with affection.

Not all scholars are agreed on who this man is. Most, in recent times, take him to be the same one who composed Song of Songs under the inspiration of God—Solomon. But I believe a better case can be made for the presence of a third character to whom this young woman had pledged her love some months before. In the interim, Solomon had seen her and had attempted to woo her to be a part of his growing harem. The Shulamite maiden refused, in spite of the persistent urgings of the other women of the court. They thought she would "have it made" if only she would give in to the king's offers of love.

But the maiden could not forget the shepherd boy to whom she had been pledged and for whom she had great love. It is to him she addresses these lines in verses 6-7. And the love the two of them had for each other was the means by which Solomon learned, with the help of the Spirit of God, about true marital love. He who had loved and lost so much was now the recipient of God's normative pattern for love, sex and marriage.

Verses 6 and 7 mark the conclusion of the book and thus set for us the purpose for which it was written. Addressing her beloved as the one she had met under the apple tree and who had awakened love in her for the first time, she requests to be placed as a seal on a cord about his neck and as a signet ring on his arm, to be his wife forever. The signet ring was worn either on the hand (Gen 41:42; Esther 3:12; Jer 22:24) or around the neck with a string through it (Gen 38:18). The seal was a mark of ownership and authority. The typical Israelite name seal was made out of stone, often pierced with a hole and worn about the neck on a cord, or occasionally on the finger as a ring. A few personal seals have been found in Israel inscribed with the words "wife of . . ." Thus, the Shulamite woman pleads for a unique relationship, to be chosen by him and to belong to him forever.

The love she describes has five elements that make it distinctive. First, it is as strong as death. Its power is as unbreakable and as irresistible as death itself. One cannot withstand it or deny it, so that it can be compared only with death—who has ever successfully withstood that power?

Second, its jealousy is as unyielding and as obdurate as the grave. The word *jealousy* has both positive and negative meanings in the Bible. When used positively, in reference to God (Ex 20:5, Deut 5:9; Ex 34:14), it suggests an undivided devotion to its object, an ardent love that brooks no rival and demands undivided attention in return. It is used in this sense in Song of Songs, pointing to a love that is jealous *for* someone, not *of* someone. Thus it is a manifestation of genuine love and protective concern. It is "cruel" or "hard" too—unyielding and resolute in its desire to be with the loved one. In the lengths to which this love will go, it is as deep, inexorable and hard as the grave.

Third, this love burns flames of fire given by the Lord himself. The word "flames" has, in Hebrew, the suffix *yah*, which must be understood as the shortened form of the name of Yahweh, the Lord (which is why I have followed the NIV marginal reading in the translation above). This love, then, does not originate solely from some carnal instinct; it emanates from the Lord himself! He is the true source of marital love. The flames of love in the heart of a man or a woman are lit by the Lord who made them. Within the bounds of marriage, the flame of love comes from the Lord.

Fourth, it is impossible to drown out this love with much water or even with a flood. Solomon had to forget trying to woo the Shulamite maiden, for all his promises of position, jewels, wealth and leisure could not drown her love for that shepherd boy back home.

Finally, such love is beyond any purchase price offered anywhere. This is the victorious side of love, and it comes from God: it cannot be bought or sold. This was not intended to condemn the custom of paying a "bride price." Such a payment was never construed as a payment "for love," nor was it used to gain love. The point, instead, was that true love from God for a man or a woman was beyond any kind of price.

Thus this text celebrates physical love within the bounds of marriage for its strength, its unquenchable nature and its source—the Lord himself.

· C H A P T E R 5 9 ·

Lucifer's Fall from Heaven

How you have fallen from heaven,
O morning star, son of the dawn!
You have been cast down to the earth,
you who once laid low the nations!
You said in your heart,
"I will ascend to heaven;
I will raise my throne
above the stars of God;
I will sit enthroned on the mount of assembly,
on the utmost heights of the sacred mountain.
I will ascend above the tops of the clouds;
I will make myself like the Most High.'
ISAIAH 14:12-14

In *a prophecy of Isaiah addressed to the king of Babylon, there is a sudden* shift from this world to a realm outside it. It describes a being with a hubris that will brook no rival and who wishes to challenge God himself for position, authority and power.

Some of the early church fathers, such as Tertullian, along with Gregory the Great and scholastic commentators, linked this prophecy in Isaiah with Luke 10:18 and Revelation 12:8. As a result, they applied the passage to the fall of Satan or Lucifer. The expositors of the Reformation era, however, would have no part of this exegesis, which they regarded as a popular perversion. The passage, in their minds, discussed human pride, not angelic—even though the pride was monumental, to be sure. Which interpretation, then, is correct? Is this passage a record of the time when Satan fell like lightning from heaven? Or is it a description of the Babylonian king only?

The key word for resolving this problem is *helel*, rendered at first as an imperative of the verb signifying "howl" ("Howl, son of the morning, for your fall"). Then it was connected with the verb *to shine* and made a derivative denoting "bright one," or more specifically "bright star," the harbinger of daybreak. The Latin term for it became *Lucifer*.

In Canaanite mythology from Ugarit, the god Athtar seems to be connected with the morning star. At one point, the gods attempted to replace Baal with Athtar, but he declined, as he found that he was unsuited for the position. The throne was too large for him. Athtar was the son of the Ugaritic god El and his wife Asherah. Athtar was the chief god in the South Arabic pantheon, known there as an astral deity, the planet Venus. In the Ugaritic world, he was known as "the terrible, awesome one" or as "the lion." Some have translated the first epithet as "a flash [of lightning]." The Ugaritic text 49, column 1, tells how his greed for power caused him to ascend the vacant throne of Baal, who had been dealt a death blow by the god of death, Mot. Assisted by his mother, he attempted to fill the vacuum left by Baal, but he was unable to do so. His feet did not reach the footstool, and his head did not clear the top of the throne. So he descended from the throne of Baal, stepping down so that "he might rule over the grand earth." Like Isaiah's Lucifer, he had aspired to ascend to a throne above the heavens but suffered a fall.

While there are a number of similarities between the Ugaritic myth and Isaiah's account, no great interpretive advantage seems to be gained by following this lead. "The mount of assembly" is parallel with Mount Zaphon or Mount Cassius in North Syria, where the gods assembled. Whether the story Isaiah tells came first or the Ugaritic myth cannot be decided from this text. Normally one would expect the real event to have been told before the mythmakers took up the tale and made secondary applications of it.

So what is the effect of all this on the interpretation? Is the story referring to the king of Babylon in hyperbolic terms, or does it refer to Satan? Normally the rules of sound interpretation demand that we assign only one interpretation to every passage; otherwise the text just fosters confusion. To make the Bible say two things at once is to make it say everything and ultimately, then, nothing.

In this situation, however, the prophet uses a device that is found often in prophetic texts: he links near and distant prophecies together under a single sense, or meaning, since the two entities, though separated in space and time, are actually part and parcel of each other.

Isaiah saw the king of Babylon as possessing an enormous amount of disgusting pride and arrogance. In cultivating aspirations that exceeded his stature and ability, he paralleled the ultimate ruler with an exaggerated sense of his own accomplishments: Satan.

Just as there was a long messianic line in the Old Testament, and everyone who belonged to that line was a partial manifestation of the one to come and yet not that one, so there was an antimessianic line of kings in the line of Antichrist and Satan. The king of Babylon was one in a long line of earthly kings who stood opposed to God and all that he stood for.

This would explain the hyperbolic language, which while true in a limited sense of the king of Babylon, applied ultimately to the one who would culminate this line of evil, arrogant kings. In this sense, the meaning of the passage is single, not multiple or even double. Since the parts belonged to the whole and shared the marks of the whole, they were all of one piece.

Just as the king of Babylon wanted equality with God, Satan's desire to match God's authority had precipitated his fall. All this served as a model for the Antichrist, who would imitate Satan and this most recent dupe in history, the king of Babylon, in the craving for power.

A similar linking of the near and the distant occurs in Ezekiel 28, where a prophecy against the king of Tyre uses the same hyperbolic language (vv. 11-19). In a similar fashion, the prophet Daniel predicted the coming of Antiochus Epiphanes (Dan 11:29-35); in the midst of the passage, however, he leaps over the centuries in verse 35 to link Antiochus Epiphanes to the Antichrist of the final day, since they shared so much as parts of the line of the antimessiah. Thus this prophetic device is well attested in the Old Testament and should not cause us special concern.

· C H A P T E R 6 0 ·

Imprisoning the Powers of Heaven and the Kings of the Earth

*In that day the LORD will punish
the powers in the heavens above
and the kings on the earth below.
They will be herded together
like prisoners bound in a dungeon;
they will be shut up in prison
and be punished [or "released"] after many days.
The moon will be abashed, the sun ashamed;
for the LORD Almighty will reign
on Mount Zion and in Jerusalem,
and before its elders, gloriously.*
ISAIAH 24:21-23

This prophecy belongs to the section known as the "Little Apocalypse" or "Little Book of Revelation" (Is 24—27) in Isaiah's great collection of messages. Here the prophet tells of a time designated as "In that day." This "day" is probably the same as the "Day of the Lord," referred to so frequently in the Old Testament. The "Day of the Lord" is a period of time that is to close our present age;

it is the time of the second coming of Christ, in judgment for all who have refused to accept him and in deliverance for all who have believed in him.

In what ways, if any, does Isaiah 24:21-23 accord with what we know of our Lord's second coming from other texts—especially from the New Testament? What is meant by the "prison" into which the celestial powers and the kings of the earth are to be herded? And why would they be "punished," or "released," after "many days"?

The vision of this chapter, which has already included the whole earth, is now enlarged further still to encompass the powers of heaven and earth. The term translated "powers" is sometimes used merely of heavenly bodies (Is 34:4; 40:26; 45:12), but at other times it is used of armies of angels (1 Kings 22:19; 2 Chron 18:18). In this case it seems to refer to the fallen angels who did not keep their first estate, but rebelled along with Satan and therefore were thrown out of heaven.

Isaiah 14 depicted the king of Babylon descending to Sheol itself in an act of rebellion. Here, both the heavenly and the earthly potentates have rebelled against God, and as a result they are to be confined to a prison (see also 2 Pet 2:4; Jude 6; Rev 20:1-3).

The time of shutting out Satan and his hosts from access to the heavenly regions is also mentioned in Revelation 12:7-17, where the dragon, in great rage, makes war with the woman and "the rest of her offspring—those who obey God's commandments and hold to the testimony of Jesus."

It has been argued that "after many days," in Isaiah 24:22, refers to the same period of time that Revelation 20:1-7 labels the "thousand years." According to John in the book of Revelation, Satan will be released from his prison at the end or conclusion of the thousand years, but just for a brief season. This would seem to correspond to the "punishing" or "releasing" of verse 22.

The word has the basic idea of "visiting," but it is a visitation for judgment; the word is used in the same way in Jeremiah 27:22. Thus, the loosing of Satan is only a prelude to his total destruction (Rev 20:10).

In this chapter Isaiah shows four judgments: (1) the judgment on the earth and the plagues that will come on humankind in the end time (parallel to the opening of the sixth seal in the book of Revelation); (2) the judgment on the world-city, or Babylon of the future; (3) the final judgment on Jerusalem and all who have dealt treacherously with Israel's remnant; and (4) the judgment that God will hold "in that day" of his second coming for all the powers of heaven and earth that have opposed him. It is this fourth judgment that is dealt with in the verses selected here (vv. 21-23).

The heavenly and earthly powers that have deceived mortals into apostasy will be visited with punishment in one and the same "day." They will be cast into the pit, only to be "visited" once more "after many days"—the millennium. Their release will not last long, for after a brief conflict, the eternal kingdom of God will come in its full glory. The millennium that has preceded this kingdom will only have prepared men and women for its majesty and glory.

· CHAPTER 61 ·

Sour Grapes That Set Children's Teeth on Edge

In those days people will no longer say,
"The fathers have eaten sour grapes,
and the children's teeth are set on edge."
Instead, everyone will die for his own sin; whoever
eats sour grapes—his own teeth will be set on edge.
JEREMIAH 31:29-30

The word of the LORD came to me: "What do you people
mean by quoting this proverb about the land of Israel:
" 'The fathers eat sour grapes,
and the children's teeth are set on edge'?
"As surely as I live, declares the Sovereign LORD,
you will no longer quote this proverb in Israel.
For every living soul belongs to me, the father as well as
the son—both alike belong to me. The soul who sins
is the one who will die."
EZEKIEL 18:1-4

The popular proverb quoted in these two passages seems to give credence to the widespread belief that people in Old Testament times were made to pay for the sins of their parents. Perhaps this idea got its start in that day, as it has continued to do so in our day, by an improper understanding of Exodus 20:5-6.

What is clear, however, is that this proverb expresses a fatalistic despair. In effect, people tended to throw up their hands and say, by way of excusing themselves of all responsibility for sin and its effects, "I can't help it. No one can fight city hall. My parents sinned; what else can you expect?"

This implication of fatalism and pleading of innocence must be faced here. The teaching of the Decalogue was that children would be affected by their parents' sin. Exodus 20:5 and Deuteronomy 5:9 carefully noted that parents did set models for their children. Sinful behaviors of parents tended to be imitated by their children. But the text never taught that the blame for the parents' sins was passed on to the children. Each person stood before God responsible for his or her own sin and faults.

A generation may have learned its errors and sins from the older generation, but it had the opportunity either to repeat those acts or to reject them and follow God's laws. Saying that "my parents [or the devil] made me do it" was not an acceptable excuse. Just as holiness could not be "caught" in the manner of a cold virus, neither could one attribute one's sin to an inescapable determinism that had programmed one to sin.

There were other errors in this thinking. The sins of the fathers, warned Moses in the Ten Commandments, would be visited on the children to the third and fourth generations. But most forgot how Moses ended that statement: that sin would extend to the third and fourth generations *of those that hated God.* In other words, when the parents hated God and their offspring followed in their steps, the devastating effects went on for three or four generations. On the other hand, for those who loved God, the effects were even mightier; for thousands of generations their descendants would reap benefits!

It is true, of course, that a person may be held responsible both as an individual and as a member of a group, even if he or she was not personally guilty in a direct way. But these alternatives were not to be confused or played off each other to excuse sin.

Group involvement led to corporate effects in the here and now. But in no sense did the Old Testament ever condone the idea that persons were saved or lost for eternity depending on what the whole group had done. Neither did it condone a fatalistic concept that once the die had been cast, there was no sense trying to do anything to remedy the situation.

Deuteronomy 24:16 stated the principle in very clear terms: "Fathers shall not be put to death for their children, nor children put to death for their fathers; each is to die for his own sin." Hence the view that personal responsibility was not known in Israel until the times of Jeremiah and Ezekiel cannot be considered correct. Nor can 2 Samuel 24, where the people were punished because of David's sin, be used as a proof of the absence of personal responsibility. In 2 Samuel 9 it is made clear that David is also punished for his own sin.

Ezekiel 18 sets up a three-generation scenario in an attempt to make clear the truth of this matter. There is first a righteous man (Ezek 18:5-9), who is followed by a wicked son (vv. 10-13), who in turn is followed by a righteous grandson (vv. 14-17). This shows that sin is not predetermined and that one need not conform to what his parents were like. Ezekiel also discusses what will happen to the wicked man if he repents of his sins and does what is right (vv. 21-23, 27), as opposed to a man who was formerly righteous and who has turned to sin (vv. 24-26; see also 33:10-16). All these alternatives are real possibilities in scriptural teaching and in everyday life.

· C H A P T E R   6 2 ·

Multitudes
Who Sleep
Will Awake

At that time Michael, the great prince who protects your people,
will arise. There will be a time of distress such as has not happened
from the beginning of nations until then. But at that time your people—
everyone whose name is found written in the book—will be delivered.
Multitudes who sleep in the dust of the earth will awake: some to
everlasting life, others to shame and everlasting contempt.
DANIEL 12:1-2

This celebrated text in Daniel is usually discussed with John 5:25-29. In many theological textbooks and commentaries, these two passages are quoted to prove that there will be a universal and simultaneous resurrection of the dead, without any distinctions or time interval between the raisings of two types of persons discussed here.

It is my contention that the passages cannot be equated, and that neither teaches, or even implies, that there is to be a simultaneous resurrection of the righteous and the wicked. In fact, the places where the two texts agree are fewer than those where

they differ. They are parallel only with respect to the first resurrection; in Daniel 12:1-3, only the resurrection of the righteous is taught. In John 5:25-29 the resurrections of *both* the righteous and the wicked are set forth, but as separate, not
simultaneous, resurrections. The error of assuming that they are
simultaneous—an error that has existed from Constantine's
day—has influenced the wording of many Christian creeds, con-
fessions and standards of faith.

The literal rendering of Daniel 12:2-3 (with an eye to its context) would go this way: "And [at that time] many [of your people, Daniel] will awake out from among the sleepers in the
ground-dust. These [who awake] will be unto everlasting life, but
those [who do not awake at that time] will be for shame and
everlasting contempt." The key point is that Daniel is not trying
to say that *all* who sleep in the dust of the earth will arise—the
two groups, "these" and "those" (or as the NIV has it, "some" and
"others"). Instead, Daniel has selected only a part, the "many"—
or "multitudes," as some prefer in an attempt to conceal the
problem I am attempting to expose.

Not everyone awakes "at that time." "At that time" (v. 1) refers
to the period during which the career of Antichrist is in force (see
the closing verses of Daniel 11) and when the fortunes of God's
covenant people Israel are being determined. This will be a "time
of distress," a term generally equated with the great tribulation.

If God's people are to be "delivered" from this time of great
distress, the implication could be a pretribulational rapture of the
church (as implied by 1 Thess 4:13-17) or to a prewrath midtrib-
ulational rapture (as one might infer from Dan 9:27). The language of Daniel 12:1-3 can be made to harmonize with either of
these views, if examined on this single point. This point must be
left open, since we can discuss it only through theological inference and not based on an exegesis of any teaching block of texts.

So not all awake "at that time," only the "many" who are fit for eternal life by virtue of having their names written in "the book [of life]."

"Those" who do not awake (and thus are not raised from the dead) at that time are the wicked dead, whom John would call the "rest of the dead" in Revelation 20:7. The reason "those" cannot be included in the resurrection of the many who "sleep in the dust of the earth" is that the verb "awake" belongs only to one class—the class of "these." In John 5:25-29, the verb "come out [of the graves]" applies to both classes, "all who are in their graves." Thus, Daniel's "many . . . out from among the sleepers" cannot mean exactly what Jesus meant by "all who are in their graves." The angel who talked with Daniel did not say that a part was the whole. Therefore, the common doctrine that teaches or implies that there is only one, universal and simultaneous resurrection for believers and unbelievers is in error. It rests on the thought that the repeated demonstrative pronoun "these" ('eleh) in Daniel refers in each case to a portion of the "many" who are raised from the dead. Actually, the "many" are just a part.

Daniel 12:1-3 is not the first reference to resurrection in the Old Testament. Resurrection has been taught already in Job 14:11-14; Job 19:25-27; Psalm 16:10; 49:15; Isaiah 25:8; 26:19; and Hosea 13:14. And, of course, there was the extraordinary revelation that this mortal flesh apparently is capable of going right into the presence of God, as in the cases of Enoch and Elijah.

· C H A P T E R 6 3 ·

How Can I Give You Up? How Can I Hand You Over?

How can I give you up, Ephraim?
How can I hand you over, Israel?
How can I treat you like Admah?
How can I make you like Zeboiim?
My heart is changed within me;
all my compassion is aroused.
I will not carry out my fierce anger,
nor will I turn and devastate Ephraim.
For I am God, and not man—
the Holy One among you.
I will not come in wrath.
HOSEA 11:8-9

The surprise in this passage is the fact that God is reluctant to give up on the northern ten tribes. While judgment had been exercised by God in the past (as in the destruction of the five cities of the plain—Sodom, Gomorrah, Admah, Zeboiim and Zobah), he definitely would not act with such fierceness here. The question is why. What made God change—for that is exactly what he had done in choosing not to impose the judgment that was richly deserved by Ephraim?

A number of texts in the Pentateuch reiterate that death and destruction will be the results of all continued disobedience. Leviticus 26:38 warns, "You will perish among the nations; the land of your enemies will devour you," and the next verse adds, "Those of you who are left will waste away." "You will quickly perish from the land" (Deut 4:26). The people would "come to sudden ruin" until they were "destroyed . . . from the land" and had "perish[ed]" (Deut 28:20-22). The perpetually disobedient could expect death (Deut 30:19), and God would "blot out their memory from mankind" (Deut 32:26).

In light of such serious threats, the gracious words of Hosea 11:8-9 are totally unexpected. How are we to reconcile the two?

The sudden shift in Hosea 11:8-9 signals new hope for Israel. The main reasons for the shift from a message of judgment to one of hope are to be found in two facts: (1) Israel would suffer a full punishment for disloyalty and would go into exile under the Assyrian conquest, and (2) the character of God, like the faces of a coin, has two sides: judgment and compassion.

In the freedom of God, he chose to deal with Israel *after* its exile under his attribute of grace and compassion. God is not like any human being whose emotions swing back and forth arbitrarily and whose wrath might suddenly turn vindictive rather than be equitable. He is God, not a man. He is the Holy One and therefore is set apart from all that is fallible, unpredictable, vacillating and arbitrary. It is his holiness that determines his difference from humans, especially in his qualities of thinking and in his moral behavior.

The passage sets up a contrast between Ephraim's stubborn, selfish rebellion and Yahweh's sovereign holiness and grace. Since God had exercised the necessary judgment for Israel's sin, he chose now to exercise his compassion and protection and to spare the people of Israel rather than obliterating them. Even though they deserved the fate of Admah and Zeboiim, he would bring them back home from captivity, just as he had promised the patriarchs in times past. God's ways are above the ways of Israel. Grace is able to overcome the shameful effects of sin. God would rescue the Israelites in spite of themselves.

The threats of Deuteronomy 4 and 30, with their parallels in Leviticus 26, were always two-sided. Judgment must come when sin has dominated, but since the covenant was a unilateral, one-sided agreement, in which only God obligated himself to fulfill its terms (while humans were not asked to take on a similar obligation), God can restore the erring party back into the agreement. Since the sin of those who had been disobedient had been dealt with, God could now deal in mercy with the new generation.

This is one of the biblical passages that most clearly reveal the heart and holiness of God. Few texts allow us to look into the character and motives of our Lord as this one does. God's heart was stirred within him (Hos 11:8; 12:6) when he thinks of how lonely, desperate and needy his people were in their exiled state. Thus he would reverse his judgment for his own name's sake.

This revelation makes this passage one of the great texts on the mercy, love and compassion of our Lord. Where sin abounded, God's grace abounded much more vigorously, overcoming even the unattractiveness and unworthiness of the recipients of that grace.

• C H A P T E R 6 4 •

Casting
Lots to Discover
Responsibility

Then the LORD sent a great wind on the sea, and such a violent
storm arose that the ship threatened to break up. All the sailors were
afraid and each cried out to his own god. . . . Then the sailors
said to each other, "Come, let us cast lots to find out who is responsible
for this calamity." They cast lots and the lot fell on Jonah.
JONAH 1:4-5, 7

T he use of "lots," or the throwing of dice, in order to discover what
is unknown seems more at home in the world of divination and
enchantment than in the biblical world of the will of God. It is
not surprising, I suppose, that these sailors would have resorted
to this means of discovery in such terrifying circumstances. But
it is surprising to learn that this method did uncover the real
culprit—that it worked. How can this fact be explained and reconciled with the rest of Scripture?

The sailors' use of divination in order to learn the source of
their problem was altogether fitting to the culture of those times.
As far as they were concerned, a storm of this intensity and

ferocity must have represented some sort of divine punishment. Someone on their ship must have angered his god in some way, they reasoned. If they were to come out of the experience alive, they had to find out who the offender was and what he had done.

As best we can tell, lots were very similar to our dice, usually with alternating light and dark sides. Some think the mysterious Urim (possibly "lights") and Thummim (possibly "darks") may have been lots used by the high priest and kept in his ephod for discerning the will of God (Ex 28:30).

The casting of lots was probably interpreted along these lines: two dark sides up meant no, while two light sides up meant yes. A combination of a light and a dark side might have meant that one should throw again. On this system, the sailors probably asked the lots "yes" or "no," taking each sailor in turn until it came Jonah's turn and the lots both came up light.

The use of lots was not altogether foreign among the people of God. At several key points in the history of Israel, lots had been used with the apparent approval and blessing of God. This may be one more case where it was not the use but the abuse of cultural tool that made it objectionable. Lots were used to determine which of the two goats would be sacrificed on the Day of Atonement (Lev 16). Joshua used lots to ferret out Achan as the guilty party after the defeat at Ai (Josh 7:14). Lots were used in the allocation of land (Josh 18—19; Ps 16:6) and in the assignment of temple duties (1 Chron 24:5). In the New Testament, our Lord's clothes were gambled for by the casting of the dice (Mt 27:35). In fact, the whole church decided between two men to fill the position left by Judas's death by the use of lots (Acts 1:15-26). True, here the casting of lots was accompanied with prayer, but my point is that lots were used. Some are fond of pointing out that all these examples were prior to Pentecost, but there seems to be no scriptural significance to such an observation.

The best way to explain the use of lots is by noting the mild endorsement expressed in Proverbs 16:33: "The lot is cast into the lap, but its every decision is from the LORD." Though this proverb is quite brief, its point seems to be that the Lord, not fate, is the reason for success, if there is any. It also seems to warn that the casting of lots does not carry with it an automatic validity, for in every case the freedom to answer lies with God, who is not at the beck and call of the thrower.

It may please God to use this means to give further confidence that one's decision, when it does not conflict with Scripture or with one's best discernment, is indeed his will. But in no sense should the casting of lots be used or viewed as a means of bypassing what can be known of God and his will through Scripture, prayer and the inner testimony of the Holy Spirit.

Accordingly, what might appear to be no more than raw superstition to a twentieth-century Westerner was an evidence of divine intervention and providence. Even the casting of lots came under the controlling eye of God.

A God Who Relents from Sending Calamity

But Jonah was greatly displeased and became angry.
He prayed to the LORD, "O LORD, is this not what I said
when I was still at home? That is why I was so quick to flee to
Tarshish. I knew that you are a gracious and compassionate God,
slow to anger and abounding in love, a God who relents
from sending calamity."
JONAH 4:1-2

So sharp is the contrast between what God had said would happen to Nineveh and what actually took place that we are left to wonder whether divine words are always fulfilled or whether God is presented as a rather fickle person in the Old Testament. Even though from the start Jonah had suspected, because of God's gracious character, that he would not carry out his threats against Nineveh, we are still left in doubt over God's ability to predict the future or his constancy of character.

Some have attempted to rescue the situation by distinguishing between God's secret will and his declared will. The former, so this line of argumentation goes, is his *real* intention, which remains fixed and unchangeable, while the latter varies depending on conditions. But this representation of God's will does not accord with Scripture elsewhere, for it still conveys the appearance of insincerity on the part of God—as if God were deceptive, representing his thoughts differently from what they really were, and representing future events differently from what he knew would eventually happen!

The language of this verse, which represents our Lord as "relent[ing]," is undoubtedly an anthropomorphism—a depiction of God in human terms. Certainly the infinite, eternal God can be known to us only through human imagery, and thus he is represented as thinking and acting in a human manner. Without anthropomorphisms, we could never speak *positively* of God; to try would be to entangle ourselves in deism, which makes God so transcendent that he is never identified with us in our world. When we rush to get rid of the human forms in our talk about God, we sink into meaningless blandness.

Nevertheless, when it comes to the eternal principles of righteousness, Scripture is just as insistent about the impossibility of change in God. Consider, for example, the declaration made to Balaam, "God is not a man, that he should lie, nor a son of man, that he should change his mind" (Num 23:19). Similarly in 1 Samuel 15:29 Samuel informs Saul, "He who is the Glory of Israel does not lie or change his mind; for he is not a man, that he should change his mind."

The descriptions of God that have to do with his inherent and immutable righteousness allow no room for change in the character of deity or in his external administrations. His righteousness calls for consistency and unchangeableness.

But such representations argue nothing against the possibility, or even the moral necessity, of a change in God's carrying out of his declarations in cases where the people against whom the judgment was issued have changed, so that the grounds for the threatened judgment have disappeared. For God *not* to change in such cases would go against his essential quality of justice and his responsiveness to any change that he had planned to bring about.

If this is the case, some wonder why the announcement made by Jonah took such an absolute form: "Forty more days and Nineveh will be overturned" (Jon 3:4). Why not plainly include "if the people do not repent"?

This objection assumes that the form given to the message was not the best suited to elicit the desired result. Actually, as the record shows, this message indeed awakened the proper response, and so the people were spared. As delivered, it was a proper account of how God felt and the danger to which Nineveh was exposed.

Of course God's warnings always carried with them the reverse side of the coin, the promises. This element of alternatives within one prophecy can be seen best in Jeremiah 18:9-11 and Ezekiel 18:24 (see, too, Rom 11:22). The good things promised in these prophecies cannot be attributed to any works righteousness or to any merited favor, but are always found in connection with the principles of holiness and human beings' obedience to God's Word.

Does this imply that all the predictions from the prophets' lips were operating under this same rule, that nothing was absolute or certain in the revealed predictive realm? Far from it! There are portions that may be regarded in the strictest sense as absolute, because their fulfillment depended on nothing but the faithfulness and power of God. Such were the declarations of Daniel about the four successive world empires. All the statements about the appearance of Christ, in his first and second advents, are included here, along with predictions about the progress of the kingdom of God and promises connected with our salvation.

But when the prophecy depicts judgment, or promises good things to come, the prophetic word is not the first and determining element; it is secondary and dependent on the spiritual response of those to whom the words are delivered.

God changed, but his character and nature as the altogether true and righteous one has never changed. As a living person, he changed only in response to a required change in the Ninevites to whom Jonah's word was delivered. Thus he exhibits no fickleness or instability. He remains the unchanging God who will withdraw his threatened judgment as soon as the human responses justify his doing so.

CHAPTER 66

Out of Bethlehem Will Come a Ruler

But you, Bethlehem Ephrathah,
though you are small among the clans of Judah,
out of you will come for me
one who will be ruler over Israel,
whose origins are from of old,
from ancient times.
MICAH 5:2

T*he difficulty attached to this verse is whether the "ruler" who is* depicted here is claimed to be both human and divine. Furthermore, is he the promised Messiah? And if he is, why does the text not link him more directly with David and his family? And what is the significance of adding the word "Ephrathah" to Bethlehem?

To answer the questions in reverse order, Ephrathah is not to be explained as the name for the environs of the village of Bethlehem. In Genesis 35:19, Ephrathah is exactly equivalent with Bethlehem. It was the older name for the same town.

But that was not the only reason for introducing the name

Ephrathah; the prophet wanted to call attention to the informing theology of the passage where these two names were first associated: Genesis 35:16-19. As in that passage, which tells of the birth of Benjamin, a new birth is about to happen. The old name Ephrathah (coming from a verb meaning "to be fruitful") is not meant to suggest the inferior things and persons in that city; instead, this town is to be most blessed, the source of fruitfulness on a grand scale for all the earth.

Bethlehem is referred to here in a masculine rather than its usual feminine form, for the prophet is viewing the city in the image of its ideal representative or personification. The city and the person are thus identified with each other.

Had the prophet intended to indicate the Bethlehem that was in Judah, not the one in Zebulon (Josh 19:15), he normally would have said "Bethlehem Judah." Obviously, he had more in mind than that, and thus the allusion to Genesis 35 seems certain.

Bethlehem's smallness in size and significance is evidenced by its omission from the list of the cities of Judah in Joshua 15 (even though some later copyists tried to amend this presumed oversight by adding it to their manuscripts).

Here is the marvel: out of a place too small to merit mention goes forth one who is to be head over Israel! But he is not called *"the* ruler," only *"a* ruler." He will be unknown and unheralded at first—merely *a* ruler. But for the moment the focus is on the idea of dominion, not on the individual.

"Out of you will come *for me"* does not refer to the prophet, but *to God.* The contrast is between human meanness and the greatness of God. Now it must be seen that it is God who is able to exalt what is small, low and inferior.

The ruler was, in the first instance, David. He sprang from these lowly roots in Bethlehem, but that was not the end of it. The promise he carried went far beyond his days and his humble origins. The soil from which Messiah sprang began in ancient times, the days of Abraham, Isaac and Jacob. Boaz, who took Ruth the Moabitess as his wife, was from Bethlehem (Ruth 2:4). David, the great-grandson of Boaz, was born in Bethlehem as well (1 Sam 16:1; 17:12).

But the conclusion of the matter will be the "days of eternity." Two Hebrew phrases, in parallel position, speak of "from ancient times" and "from days of eternity." The first refers to the distant past, the second to the actions that God initiated from before time began and that will last into eternity future. The sending of the Messiah was not an afterthought; it had been planned from eternity. In other words, Messiah existed before his temporal birth in Bethlehem. His eternity is thus contrasted with all the days of the Bethlehem families through which line he eventually came, as regards his human flesh.

The Hebrew 'olam, "eternity," is used in connection with either God himself or the created order. While it can just mean "ancient times" within history, given the contrast here with the early beginnings of David in olden days, the meaning that best fits the context would be a reference to Christ's preexistence. Thus, our Lord came in the line of David (2 Sam 7:8-16; Ps 89:35-37), yet he was one with the Father from all eternity.

They Will Look on Me Whom They Have Pierced

And I will pour out on the house of David and the inhabitants
of Jerusalem a spirit of grace and supplication. They will look
on me, the one they have pierced, and they will mourn for him as one
mourns for an only child, and grieve bitterly for him as one
grieves for a firstborn son.
ZECHARIAH 12:10

Does this text teach, or even imply, that there will be two comings of Messiah to earth? Few texts have been cited in Jewish-evangelical discussions more than this one. And if one were to search the Old Testament for evidence that Christ would come twice, this is probably the only text that could be used.

At the heart of debate over this verse are the following questions. Is the subject of the verb "look" the same as the subject of "pierce"? Is "me" to be equated with "him" in verse 10? Are those who participated in the piercing the same ones who in the eschatological day will look on him and grieve bitterly? One final problem is this: is it possible to pierce God, who is spirit?

Naturally, God is spirit and not corporeal flesh. That is taught not only in John 4:24 but also in Isaiah 31:3. The mystery of this Zechariah passage is that the speaker of verse 10 is Yahweh himself. He is the one who will pour out grace and supplication on the house of Israel and David. Moreover, the first person occurs over and over again in this chapter (vv. 2, 3, 4, 6, 9 and 10), but in every case it refers to the Messiah, the one who is pictured as one with God himself. In fact, Zechariah 11 says that Yahweh's representative, the Good Shepherd, will be rejected. Thus, one can only conclude that it is the Messiah who is divine and who will be rejected and pierced. However, he will be deeply mourned at some time in the future and then finally appreciated by all those who had previously rejected him.

"On that day" (v. 11), when Messiah is restored to rightful recognition by all those who formerly rejected his person and work, he will return to restore paradisiacal conditions. Most Jewish interpreters will concede that there will indeed be such a coming of Messiah—when there will be peace. They insist, however, that he could not have come previously.

That is precisely where this text comes into play. If it is agreed that the context has to do with Messiah's coming when there is peace, then it must be recognized that he has at some previous time been pierced. When did this happen? And by whom? And for what? Only the Christian claims for Jesus of Nazareth can fit the details of this passage.

Others have seen the irresistible force of this argument and therefore have sought to show a switch in pronoun antecedents in the middle of the verse. This interpretation makes the people of Israel the ones looking, but the nations are the ones piercing. Since the two occurrences of "they" are separated in the text solely by the prepositional phrase "on me" and the pronominal expression "whom" ("the one" in NIV), it would be most unnatural to assume that the antecedent has changed. The only reason for doing so would be to avoid the obvious force of the statement.

The New Jewish Publication Society's translation *Tanakh: The Holy Scriptures* (1988) has rendered this verse a bit more smoothly: "But I will fill the House of David and the inhabitants of Jerusalem with a spirit of pity and compassion; and *they shall lament to Me about those who are slain*, wailing over them as over a favorite son and showing bitter grief as over a first-born" (emphasis mine—to point out the section where the problem occurs).

The problem with this translation is that it breaks the rules of Hebrew grammar to avoid the obvious implications of this Hebrew verse. It turns the active form of "pierce" into passive, and the subjects into objects; and this the Hebrew will not allow! It is a heroic effort to bypass the logical implication that the one who speaks is the one who was pierced by those who now stare in amazement in the eschatological, or future, day.

Other Jewish interpreters have given up and have instead found here a case for two Messiahs: Messiah son of Joseph, who did in fact suffer, and Messiah son of David, who did not suffer, but who is to come in glory and power to rule at a time when peace comes on earth. This is a late invention, created in response to the claims of the Christian movement.

Messiah has already come once. He suffered on the cross for our sin. He will come again in power and with glory.

· CHAPTER 6 8 ·

I the Lord Do Not Change

I the LORD do not change.
So you, O descendants of Jacob,
are not destroyed.
MALACHI 3:6

The major difficulty with this passage is understanding what is meant by the claim that God never changes. Does this assertion mean that God is impassible—that he is without any emotions? Is he then basically inflexible, incapable of yielding on any point once he has set in motion a decision to act in a certain way? And if he is able to respond to any legitimate changes in his creatures, then what does it mean to claim that he is unchanging? Isn't the boast, at that point, a liability?

This question, like the earlier question about the problem of the anger of God, raises the problem of divine passibility (God's capacity to feel, suffer, be angry or respond to humans and events). The second-century heresy of Gnosticism took strong exception to any claim that God could feel, experience, suffer or respond to things at all. Instead, God was seen as impassible, entirely free of all affections and emotions and altogether apathetic. The most famous advocate of this wrongheaded position was Marcion.

Malachi 3:6 is not the only text that claims that God is unchangeable. Balaam was told the same truth in Numbers 23:19: God was not a man that he should repent. First Samuel 15:29 repeats the same claim, and James 1:17 says that there is no variableness or shadow of turning in the Father of lights.

However, whenever men and women responded to God's Word, either for good or for ill, then God is said to have changed in a corresponding way. So which is true? Is there no change, or is there constant change in the Godhead?

The problem of change in God can be answered best by noting that with respect to God's essence, attributes, moral character and determination to punish sin and reward goodness, there can be no variation or inconsistency. With regard to these characteristics, there is absolute and unconditional dependability.

Behind Malachi's solemn assurance is the assumption that some may doubt the truthfulness of this statement. The tense of the verb in Hebrew stresses this truth as a fact of the past as well as one that has significance for the present.

Because God remains dependable, the descendants of Jacob had not been destroyed. Israel's continued existence was due to God's unchangeable love and mercy. Had not God promised that he would never violate his covenant with Abraham and David (Ps 89:34)? Thus no vacillation or lack of dependability could be found in the living Lord. The same unchangeableness, with regard to his judgment, can be seen in Jeremiah 4:28; 15:6; 20:16; Ezekiel 24:14; Hosea 13:14 and Zechariah 8:14, while the resoluteness of his being, as seen in his love, is stressed in Psalm 110:4 and Hosea 11:8-9.

The changes attributed to God have to do only with his mode of dealing with mortals, when they had pulled away from his purposes or ways. God, as a living person, has the qualities of personality, freedom and holiness. Therefore, if he is to remain constant in his character and person, he must change his actions toward those who violate what he stands for. If we, as humans, can change in our response to situations in order to remain consistent with our true nature, then it should not be irreconcilably difficult to see God doing the same for even higher purposes, and with what is evidently a higher respect for his own holy nature and being.

Scripture Index